FAITH AND FREEDOM

THE CHRISTIAN FAITH ACCORDING TO THE LUTHERAN CONFESSIONS

CHARLES S. ANDERSON

AUGSBURG PUBLISHING HOUSE
Minneapolis, Minnesota

*To my mother and father, Guro and Sam—
who taught me the substance of the faith by
their words, and its meaning by their lives.*

FAITH AND FREEDOM

Copyright © 1977 Augsburg Publishing House

Library of Congress Catalog Card No. 76-27087

International Standard Book No. 0-8066-1558-3

Scripture quotations unless otherwise noted are from the Re-
vised Standard Version of the Bible, copyright 1946, 1952, and
1971 by the Division of Christian Education of the National
Council of Churches.

MANUFACTURED IN THE UNITED STATES OF AMERICA

Contents

Abbreviations

B.C. Book of Concord (page references are to the edition edited by Theodore G. Tappert

A.C. Augsburg Confession

Apol. Apology to the Augsburg Confession

S.A. Smalcald Articles

P.P. Treatise on the Power and Primacy of the Pope

S.C. Small Catechism

L.C. Large Catechism

F.C. Formula of Concord

F.C.S.D. Formula of Concord, Solid Declaration

F.C.Ep. Formula of Concord, Epitome

Preface

In a time when relativism is common in all areas of life, there is a rising concern and interest in the values of the past and their possible relevance to the present. In a mass society persons are increasingly faced with problems of identity and meaning. Most of all there is a continuing concern for the gospel, that promise which became flesh in Jesus Christ, and which calls all persons to a forgiven past, to an ever-new present, and to an open future.

What you have before you is meant to aid you in reaching some understanding of these matters, and in finding some answers for the questions of our day. Careful reading of the confessional documents will be of great value as you work through this study. The Tappert edition of the Book of Concord is especially useful. The Augsburg Confession and the Small Catechism are also available separately.

The substance of this book will be recognizable to the several generations of students I have taught at Luther Seminary, St. Paul, Minnesota. Their continuing comments and evaluations have helped give shape to the discussion. I am indebted to them. Two other persons, Drs. George Aus and Herman Preus, my teachers, later my colleagues, always my friends and brothers in Christ, wander through these pages, correcting and encouraging. They have not read and reacted to what I have written, however, and so cannot be identified with it or held responsible for it. Finally, a thanks which cannot really be spoken is here given to my wife, Catherine, without whom neither this study nor anything else would have real meaning or joy for me.

CHARLES S. ANDERSON

1

The
Story of the
Lutheran Confessions

Theologians do not live in a vacuum, cut off from the pressures, pleasures, and pains of life. They, and the documents from their pens, can only be understood in the setting of their times and concerns. It is necessary for us, therefore, to describe briefly the context of the Lutheran Confessions. Only when we combine a picture of their era with an understanding of our own can we make some judgment about the value and applicability of the Confessions today.

The standard collection of Lutheran confessional documents known as the *Book of Concord* appeared in 1580. In addition to materials from the sixteenth century it contains three statements from the early years of the Christian community, the Apostles', Nicene, and Athanasian creeds. The Lutherans claimed these as their own and insisted that they represented their position, to emphasize, first of all, their ties to the past. They accepted the ancient heritage and were building upon it. They also wished to underline the fact that they were not heretic or heterodox in belief, but were a part of the

entire universal, catholic church of Christ. This emphasis also would serve as a needed defense against persecution. They were to have enough theological and political trouble without having the additional, unnecessary
task of demonstrating that they were orthodox on central
matters, such as the doctrines of Christ and the Trinity.

The Apostles' Creed

The Apostles' Creed comes to us from sometime after
A.D. 400. At this time a text which is essentially the same
as the present one was used by a person named Rufinus.
In the eighth century a writer named Priminius presents the exact text we have today. It is evident that the
creed is "apostolic" in content, not in authorship.

How did this statement evolve? How did the church
move from the early, very simple assertions that "Jesus
is Messiah" and "Christ is Lord" to the comparative
complexity of this later form? We assume that as the
church developed nearly every congregation had its own
rudimentary form of a creed. There are glimpses of such
early creeds about A.D. 180 in the writings of Tertullian
and Irenaeus, but the first example of a formalized statement comes from Hippolytus of Rome around 197. Here
we have affirmation of the congregation of Rome. It is
trinitarian in organization and has most of the material
found later in the Apostles' Creed.

Creeds are always formed in the context of controversy.
We give but one example. During the early days of the
community certain individuals, influenced primarily by
Greek thought, began to question the reality of the
humanity of Jesus. Since he was God among us and God
was absolutely holy, while in their view the created
world was absolutely evil, it was not possible that Jesus
truly assumed flesh and was God incarnate. He only

seemed to be human. The name for this position is *Docetism* from the Greek *dokeō*, "to appear, to seem."

The earlier christological statement, "Jesus is Lord" did not address this problem. What biblical affirmations could be inserted into the creed to make certain that Docetism was recognized as being in error? In the Apostles' Creed the words, "born . . . suffered . . . died" all have reference to the reality of the incarnation, and thus are refutations of Docetism. The entire document can be seen to have developed in this way, as response and corrective to aberrant positions.

Of the ancient creeds the Apostles' is perhaps the most widely used today. In contrast to the other two ecumenical creeds, which contain concepts and words drawn from extra-biblical material, the Apostles' Creed is rather simple and biblical. A second strength is that it emphasizes God's action rather than venturing into analysis of ultimate reality. It speaks about what God *has done* and *is doing* among his people, rather than probing into the inner workings of the Trinity. In its brevity and simplicity it is unsurpassed for catechetical and liturgical use.

The Apostles' Creed has some shortcomings, however. Its basic affirmations were not sufficiently detailed for later controversies. The saving work of Christ, *why* he came, is not clearly put, but only implied. Various explanations to the Apostles' Creed, the Small Catechism, for example, fill this need.

The Nicene Creed

The Nicene Creed is the product of two councils, one in 325, the second in 381. It addresses the issue of the relationship of the Father and the Son in the Trinity.

A controversy had developed in the city of Alexandria in the early 300s. One party, led by Arius, had argued that the Son or Logos, while certainly God for us and the creator of the universe, is nonetheless himself a created being and not essentially divine. "There was a time," their motto went, "when he was not." Against this group another formed, led by a young man named Athanasius. Followers of Athanasius maintained that salvation can come only from God himself, who became incarnate. It could not depend upon some created, intermediary being. In addition, they insisted that the Arians were in error by holding that some intermediary being had created the world. God maintains personal and perpetual contact with his creation. "The world," as an earlier theologian named Irenaeus had put it, "is able to bear the hand of the father." The basic question remained: Is Jesus Christ God, or simply a created being, although God for us?

By the time this controversy became public, Christianity had in effect become the state religion of the empire. Constantine, the emperor, did not wish to have theological strife disturbing the peace and called a council to meet at Nicaea to settle the matter. The creed of the congregation of Caesarea was proposed for adoption, and some additions were made which addressed the issue directly. In the second article the words directed against the Arian position included: "the only begotten Son of God, begotten of the Father before all ages, God of God, Light of Light, very God of very God, begotten not made, being of one substance with the Father, through whom all things were made . . ." (B.C., p. 18).

The controversy did not end at Nicaea, but continued for another 50 years. The creed was slightly amended at Constantinople in 381 and assumed a central place in the expressions of faith of the church. It is long enough for its theological purpose and short enough for liturgical use. It does not explain, but affirms, the relationship between Father and Son. This was a necessary formulation in order to adhere to the biblical pictures and to prevent Christianity from becoming another polytheistic system.

The Nicene Creed has certain difficulties for some persons. One is its use of non-biblical language. Another is its relative complexity of thought and a metaphysical thrust not found in the Apostles' Creed. This is characteristic of Eastern Christianity, which has always been more metaphysical, philosophical, and speculative than the theology of the Western church. There is also a certain heaviness in expression, and even obscurity. It did not answer all the questions, but provided a needed statement for that time. It has continued to express the place of the Son in the Trinity in a helpful manner.

The Athanasian Creed

The Athanasian Creed is far less familiar to most Christians than either of the other two. In fact most persons are not even aware of its existence. The name of the great controversialist of Nicaea is attached to this statement, but he did not write it. It is never mentioned by either Athanasius or his contemporaries, nor at the Councils of Ephesus (431) or Chalcedon (451). It does not contain the discussion of the "one substance" so important in the Nicaean statement and in Athanasius' whole career and writing. One indication of its Western origin is the phrase "and the Son" in reference to the procession of the Holy Spirit. The Eastern church has never accepted this addition.

This third creed addresses questions raised about the Trinity and the person of Christ. The basic formulation is related to that adopted at the Council of Chalcedon in 451, which attempted to avoid both separation and merger of the two natures of Christ. The furthest the church has come in this debate is to affirm the existence of the two natures while denying that they are merged or separated. Both are present in all that our Lord does on our behalf.

The documents included in the specifically Lutheran Confessions originating in the sixteenth century were written over a span of nearly fifty years (1529-1577) and by many different persons. Most of the great and formative personal battles of the Reformation had already been fought by Luther and others and now the insights and conclusions of these struggles were to be formulated in statements of faith which became the confession of the community in its times of controversy. A brief review of the titles, authors, and situations of the documents is necessary. We will follow the order in which they appear in the Book of Concord.

The Augsburg Confession (1530)

In early 1530 the Emperor, Charles V, summoned the various lords and representatives of the free cities of the Holy Roman Empire to an assembly in Augsburg, Germany. The meeting was to convene in April with the expressed intention of settling the religious debates shaking the empire. Charles wanted peace so that there might be one church, one expression of the faith, and also unity in facing the military pressures of both France and the Turks.

Many of the representatives brought leading theologians with them to Augsburg. Luther came as far south as Coburg, the edge of his ruler's territory, where he waited while his colleagues moved on. His safety depended on staying in Saxony, for he had been declared an outlaw by the Emperor in 1521. The task of writing a

summary of the evangelical faith as held in Saxony therefore fell to Philip Melanchthon, although Luther maintained lengthy and detailed correspondence with him.
Melanchthon, Luther's younger colleague at Wittenberg
and a noted humanist, also made use of several documents in his writing. These included articles prepared
at meetings in Torgau (1530), Schwabach (1529), and
Marburg (1529). In addition, articles written for the
visitation of parishes in Saxony (1528) and a major
work by Luther on the Lord's Supper (1528) were used
as resource material.

The Confession was read on June 25, 1530, as the position of seven princes and two free cities. Later there
were more signatures, and the document assumed the
character of an official statement of faith.

It is basically an ecumenical, irenic, and conservative
statement, emphasizing continuity with the historic
church while noting in particular differences with other
groups that had turned away from Rome. The central
affirmation is found in the fourth article which deals
with how relationship with God is established (justification by grace through faith).

The Apology to the Augsburg Confession (1531)

The Apology is an explanation and elaboration of
parts of the Augsburg Confession, written by Melanchthon and occasioned by a response to the original statement made by Roman Catholic theologians at the order
of the Emperor. This Roman Catholic document was
known as the *Confutation.*

The Apology is much more detailed and polemic than
the earlier statement. Even Melanchthon, still the most
amicable of the Lutheran leaders, had been angered by
parts of the Roman *Confutation.* Rather than simply

stating a position, the Confessors made extensive use of supporting documentation from the Scriptures and the fathers. Once again the central thrust was on justification by grace through faith.

The Smalcald Articles (1537)

These were written by Luther for discussion by the German secular leaders and theologians in preparation for a council of the church called by Pope Paul III to meet in the spring of 1537.

The preparatory meeting was held in February 1537 at Smalcald. The articles were not discussed or voted upon because of Luther's absence (he was seriously ill) and Melanchthon's arguments against them. He felt they were too harsh, especially on the Lord's Supper, a topic of negotiation between this ever tranquil leader and some south German groups.

The *Articles* are a very forthright and unequivocal statement of the Lutheran position. Melanchthon was correct in seeing them as a poor foundation for building a compromise or for fostering conciliation. They were later given general acceptance as a clear exposition of the essentials of the Lutheran understanding. A treatise by Melanchthon on *The Power and the Primacy of the Pope* (1537) was appended to them. In the treatise, which was harsher than usual for this theologian, papal power was acknowledged to exist by human power rather than divine right, but its limitations and errors were forcefully enumerated.

The Small Catechism and the Large Catechism

The documents were written by Luther and published in 1529. Both Roman Catholics and Protestants were deeply concerned with the education of clergy and laity. A visit to many parishes in Saxony had convinced Luther and his colleagues that something had to be done to improve the situation.

The Large Catechism was meant to be a "brief compend and summary of all of Holy Scripture," and in this sense "preaching for children" and "the Bible of the laity." The Small Catechism is a positive, serene statement; a beautiful summary of an evangelical position.

The two statements were gradually received by the Lutherans as confessional documents. In the internal controversies after Luther's death in 1546 they were sometimes used to correct and attack Melanchthon.

The Formula of Concord (1577)

This was prepared during a three-year period and published in 1577. It was occasioned by serious internal theological controversies that threatened the Lutheran family. A major split had developed between those who felt they were following the insights of Luther and those who saw Melanchthon as the more reliable guide to understanding the older reformer. Extreme positions were developed on both sides. Gradually a third, mediating party appeared, led by persons like James Andreae and Martin Chemnitz. Their efforts finally prevailed, and the extremist positions on both sides were rejected and the relatively brief statements of the earlier documents were developed in some detail. The intention was to remain true to the Scriptures and the earlier confessional statements.

In 1580, fifty years to the day after the reading of the Augsburg Confession, the *Book of Concord* was placed on sale. The documents it contains have provided the basic confessional reference point for Lutheran Christians ever since.

2

The Need for Confessional Writings

We are a people with a past, a history, and a name. Picture what it must mean to a child to be lost in a huge store, without a name, or to be a person suffering from amnesia, lying in a hospital, without name or memory. No identity, no past, and therefore, no future. A song put it, "We didn't know who we were, we didn't know what we did. We were just on the road." In contrast to this we are reminded by the Scripture that "once you were no people, but now you are God's people" (1 Peter 2:10). And, "Fear not, for I have redeemed you; I have called you by name, you are mine" (Isaiah 43:1). We have been given a name; we are known; we belong to a family, a covenant people that has a past and a future. The heritage of the past can be studied, its wisdom appropriated. This is one of our tasks.

It is one thing to study the past; it is quite another to live in it. We are not about to begin a trip through a museum. We must read critically, aware that those who went before us were persons of both wisdom and error, of insight and failure. We are called to build on the past, and move on. Those without an awareness of history are condemned to repeat its errors. Conversely, it is not necessary to rediscover the insights of past ages in each succeeding generation. We must make them our own to be sure, but we need not "start from scratch" in each lifetime.

There are two themes, therefore, in this study and in the Confessions themselves—continuity and newness. Some things have not changed appreciably. As the confessional writers looked at the history of the race, they concluded that the basic problem had not changed: the problem was still mankind. The basic answer, to their perception, had not changed: it was Jesus Christ who is the same yesterday and today and for ever (Hebrews 13:8).

They also asserted, as we must, that there is newness. There are new times, new opportunities, new expressions, and challenges, but always in the midst of flux and change there is some continuity.

The documents we will be studying are called "confessions." This word may be used in three ways: it can refer to a confession of sin, to a public testimony characterized by praise of God, or to a written confession of faith, a creed. When we speak of the Lutheran Confessions, we refer primarily to written creeds or statements of faith, although in all such statements there is certainly also the recognition of sin and the praise of the works of God.

One more thing about the statements: they are not private or individual expressions, but rather the official, collective voice of the church. As such they help describe what it means to belong to a particular part of the Christian family. They have a central role in preaching, teaching, and living within the continuing heritage of the Reformation.

Problems in Studying the Confessions

In our study certain problems will become apparent. For one thing, the language and concepts used are often so time-conditioned as to require translation. The sixteenth century was an era of great theological battles; it was a time of polemics. There are controversies today, to be sure, but the fronts have often shifted, and the tone of the debate has grown less harsh. For example, few today believe that the papacy is the anti-Christ, but this charge is made in the documents of the Reformation era. Our task is to separate the positive principles, the continuing significant material, from the polemical sections or those which address issues that either no longer exist or that persevere in different form.

Another problem relates to our own context. Ours is an ecumenical age, a time of appreciation of other traditions. It is possible to meet other Christians with the open hand of friendship rather than the closed fist of controversy. To some, this context means that confessional concern is a thing of the past and that what is needed now is a blending of previously conflicting traditions. This is an anti-confessional time for them. I do not agree. Healthy ecumenism results from a sharing of strengths, not a merging of weaknesses; we are all enhanced and built up when the insights we have preserved are shared with each other. We cannot opt for a lowest common denominator at the expense of the message of the Scriptures. We look rather for a process of mutual enrichment and correction whose goal is the unity of faith of which our Lord speaks (John 10:16; 17:22).

One of the central confessional statements, the Augsburg Confession, clearly indicates this type of ecumenical concern as it emphasizes the ties to the historic church. It was the author's conviction that the signers were in the tradition of the whole church. At one point he notes, "As can be seen, there is nothing here that departs from the Scriptures or the catholic church or the church of Rome, insofar as the ancient church is known to us from its writers" (A.C. XXI, p. 47).

This document is peaceful, irenic in character, and aims primarily at sharing insights rather than attacking opponents. Certain other of the Lutheran documents, like the Smalcald Articles, are more of an argumentative nature, but the overall tone of the collection is ecumenical.

A final problem to be noted has to do with the question of truth and the possibility of conveying it by means of sentences and propositions. While the Confessors did work for accuracy and precision in language and were concerned that their argumentation move logically and clearly, they were not in total agreement with some of their contemporaries, or with some in our day, on a basic understanding of the nature of truth and the function of language. Truth, for them, was essentially in a person, in God. To be true was to be in relationship with this person. One knows the truth, not by scientific analysis, moving from the particular to the general, but by revelation of a person and his will.

Words, then, cannot encompass or contain the truth. At best they are pictures that point beyond themselves to another. Think of the words used to describe God in the Scriptures: God is a farmer, a warrior, a king, a general, a shepherd. These are descriptions, not logical analyses; they are windows that give only a glimpse of a reality that will not be tied down or summarized by our words and concepts.

How does one apprehend or grasp the truth? The Confessors did not play down the significance of rational inquiry, but understood that the truth which resides in a person and that confronts us in the promises of that person, is to be grasped not by intellectual inquiry, but by faith. This truth is revealed, and is to be apprehended only by faith.

Finally, what is the relation between truth and error? If truth is essentially a matter of the correspondence of language and reality, if it is reached by logical analysis and is communicated by words that correspond to that reality, then error is handled by further analysis and calm discourse. If truth resides in a person and in relationship with that person, then to be in error is to be outside of that circle; it is refusal to believe, to have faith. The relationship between the two is not one of calm discourse but of pitched battle. Two persons illustrate the two approaches to this matter: Erasmus, the prince of the humanists, and his opponent, Luther. Erasmus, calm, discursive, logical; Luther, passionate, argumentative, and often polemical.

The significance of this disagreement on the nature of truth, language and apprehension will be apparent many times in this study.

The Confessions in Outline

In studying the Lutheran Confessions we will organize our analysis around the heart of the Lutheran position, i.e., we will see how the Confessions answer the basic question of justification by faith or of how a person becomes right with God, how relationship with God is reestablished. With this as our center we will see how other concerns fall into place. For example, what is the basis for the gracious act of justification? Why is it needed? What means does God use to effect this new relationship? What are its results? Finally, what errors in theology and church practice can be traced to a misunderstanding of this basic article? In each instance the related concerns will be studied in dialog with the central article. The whole effort can be diagrammed like this:

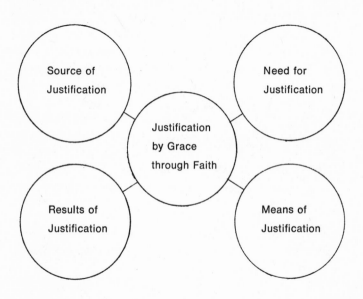

Source of
Justification

Need for
Justification

Justification
by Grace
through Faith

Results of
Justification

Means of
Justification

Sources of Confessions

How do statements of faith and praise come into being?

On the most basic level they spring from the urge of faith to express itself. It is true that, "Out of the abundance of the heart the mouth speaks" (Matthew 12:34). Whether in an individual or in a church, faith is the source of confession. Faith, the gift of God born through the work of the Holy Spirit, brings a ferment within which bubbles forth and strives for expression. This was the experience of the earliest followers of Jesus when they recognized, sometimes belatedly, that he was the Christ. Nathaniel exclaims, "Rabbi, you are the Son of God! You are the King of Israel" (John 1:49). Peter says, "Lord, to whom shall we go? You have the words of eternal life; and we have believed and have come to know that you are the Holy One of God" (John 6:68-69). Martha confesses, "Yes, Lord; I believe that you are the Christ, the Son of God, he who is coming into the world" (John 11:27). Thomas says simply, "My Lord and my God!" (John 20:28). The common point in all such expressions is that they are spontaneous and informal confessions which flow from an overflowing heart.

These simple affirmations provide in skeleton form what later would become a formal statement of recognition in the Christian community, a password for admission into the church. The one article of faith of the early Chrisians was "Jesus is Messiah," the Son of God. Baptisms recorded in Acts are on the basis of confession of faith. Christ had to be known and confessed. One believed in the heart and confessed with the lips (Romans 10:10).

Later on the very brief christological statements (cf. for example 1 Corinthians 12:3; Mark 8:30) would be expanded to a trinitarian formula as in Matthew 28, where baptism is in the name of the Father, Son and Holy Spirit.

At times the confession is bipartite as in Romans where the apostle brings "grace and peace from God the Father and our Lord, Jesus Christ" (Romans 1:6; see also 1 Timothy 2:5ff.; Romans 4:24; 1 Peter 1:21).

The second source of confession is like the first in that it springs from faith, but it is not spontaneous and it is corporate rather than individual. Here confession is the response of the church, the community of believers to God, to the gospel. It is as if God's self-revelation is now met by the community's reply, by the corporate confession, "I believe." This is what happens each Sunday morning in the service. There is a progression, a movement in public worship: preparation in the Old Testament reading, interpretation in the Epistle, and the announcement of the promise of God in the Gospel. In a sense God speaks, he reveals his saving purpose in Jesus Christ, and then almost as if Christ were once again questioning his followers, "Who do men say that I am?, "Who do you say that I am?" The congregation answers, "I believe . . . in God, the Father, Son and Holy Spirit." This is a high point in the service, the congregation's response, the church's answer, her confession of faith. A confession in this sense is a holy thing. The Apostles' and Nicene creeds, the Augsburg Confession are examples of the voice of the holy Christian church saying, "Amen. Truly it is so. You can depend on it" to the Lord of the church.

A confession of faith is a holy thing. In some churches the worshipers kneel, incline, or bow at the words of the Nicene Creed, ". . . and was made man." Luther's attitude toward this practice is clear in a comment he made.

The following tale is told about a coarse and brutal lout. While the words, "And was made man" were being sung in church, he remained standing, neither genuflecting nor removing his hat. He showed no reverence, but just stood there like a clod. All the others dropped to their knees when the Nicene Creed was prayed and chanted devoutly. Then the devil stepped up to him and hit him so hard it made his head spin.

He cursed him gruesomely and said: "May hell consume you, you boorish ass! If God had become an angel like me and the congregation says: 'God was made an angel,' I would bend not only my knees but my whole body to the ground! Yes, I would crawl ten ells down into the ground. And you vile human creature, you stand there like a stick or a stone. You hear that God did not become an angel but a man like you, and you just stand there like a stick of wood!" Whether this story is true or not, it is nevertheless in accordance with the faith. With this illustrative story the holy fathers wished to admonish the youth to revere the indescribably great miracle of the incarnation; they wanted us to open our eyes wide and ponder these words well.[1]

Now I am not recommending that you incline during the confession of faith, although bodily action often is an aid to more complete understanding and expression of religious truth. What we are illustrating is the character of confessions of faith as responses to the good news of God. They are precious to the church and are to be approached with reverence. In many instances they are stained with blood; people have died confessing them and the Christ to which they point.

This presents another problem for our type of study: confessions are meant to be confessed, not analyzed, just as liturgies are meant to be prayed and not dissected. Our analysis and discussion will put us into an artificial setting. We will be helped only by keeping the theme of holiness before us.

A third characteristic of confessions is that they are always born in controversy. They are documents of defense or offense. They spring from periods in which the church was forced to clarify and define its faith in the face of hostile and in some instances aberrant forces. Watch for this as you read them. However they may sound to us, insulated as we are by several hundred years, these are documents of battle; they are flags and banners for combat. No smoke-filled committee rooms here, peopled by doddering old lawyers looking for a peaceful compromise. There is rather a passionate concern for the truth which is in, and is, Jesus Christ. When the Augsburg Confession was read, one of the German princes who supported the position of the document replied to the implied threat of the Emperor with the words, "I will lose my life and my land rather than deny my Christ." This is the spirit of confession.

The Function of Confessions Today

We know that confessional statements have played an important role in the creation, preservation, and identification of the church in the past. How should we regard them today?

For some people, the documents are a body of legally binding statements. While not held on the same level as the Scripture, they nonetheless convey God's truth in propositional form, free from inadequacy and historical contingency. This purity of thought and expression is characteristic of the whole period during which the Confessions were written.

Another way of expressing this legal view is to require unconditional subscription to the Confessions because they are seen to be the doctrinal decisions of the Holy Scripture itself. Scripture is to be interpreted on the basis of the Confessions, and not vice versa. In this way some hope to guarantee that all interpret Scripture as the church does. Since all doctrines are based on the clear teaching of the statements of Scripture, confessional subscription covers all doctrines.

If one shares in the view that confessions are basically legal documents that somehow adequately convey the truths of Scripture and cover nearly every situation, then their proper use is that of an authoritative model for life and action to which one turns in nearly every problem. They are basically laws.

The opposite extreme to the legal view is one which sees confessions as basically collections of historical artifacts that are of interest in telling us what Luther and his contemporaries were about. They have no contemporary relevance. For those of this persuasion a study of the documents is like a tour through a museum, where one examines the curiosities, exclaims, "Wasn't that interesting?" and then wanders on.

Many hold this view today, not all of them for the same reasons. Some are of a liberal, non-confessional mind set. They want to leap over the Confessions and get back to Luther. Having made the jump, they often proceed to take bits and pieces of the Reformer and so prove just about anything they wish. But there is a difference between the writings of Luther the individual, and those which have assumed confessional status. Not everything Luther penned has become confessional. A confession is something that has been adopted by the assembly of believers. It is their corporate statement. Some of Luther's writings were adopted in this way, for example, the two catechisms and the Smalcald Articles. Others of his writings were not adopted and are valuable for giving us increased insight into the man and his times, but they do not bind or inform us in the same way as the corporate voice of the church. The distinction between a private writing and the corporate statement of the church is an important one and must be maintained.

Some have difficulty seeing any contemporary relevance of the statements because they are convinced that the situation is so different that there is no real connection. They say, "If the situation were the same today, I would hold to their position." Here one accepts the documents *insofar as* they correspond to the Scriptures and speak to our times. Each person then tends to become his or her own judge of what is confessional.

Still others are openly anti-confessional in their approach. They apply tests of piety and pragmatism to the documents and are often not helped by the results. These statements of faith are not the same as the Scriptures, but they are of great value as witnesses to the Scriptures. They do not enrich and enrapture in the same way as the original texts do, nor do they give much help in raising budgets or planning parish programs. This does not mean that they are without value in the church. Those who believe that they should be skipped over in favor of the Scriptures, who wish to make us choose one or the other, frequently belong to a broader anti-theological and anti-intellectual party in the church. They are missing an important point and thus impoverishing their ministries.

Now obviously I disagree with those for whom the Confessions are legal documents or historical artifacts. But these are not the only options. It is more helpful to see the Confessions as *pointers, treasures* and *anchors.*

The Confessions are *pointers.* In a refreshingly un-self-conscious manner they point beyond themselves to the Scriptures. They insist, "that the prophetic and apostolic writings of the Old and New Testaments are the only rule and norm according to which all doctrines and teachers alike must be appraised and judged" (F.C.Ep. p. 464; see also p. 505).

According to the Confessions the Scriptures themselves have a pointing function; they point beyond themselves to their center, to Christ. Whenever I think of the Confessors and their self-understanding as pointers to the Scriptures and to Jesus Christ, I think of a painting by Matthias Grünewald, a picture of the crucified Christ with some onlookers standing by. One of the watchers is John the Baptist who is pointing at the central figure. If you look at the figure of John carefully, you will note that something is wrong with the picture. The pointing finger on the hand raised toward Jesus is elongated out of proportion. This was the artist's way of showing John's self-perception: "He must increase, but I must decrease" (John 3:30). The Confessors stand in that tradition of pointing beyond themselves.

Secondly, the Confessions are *treasures*. They are a part of the living tradition of the church. They are a part of what the New Testament period called the *paradosis,* the root word of which means "to hand over the goods, to deliver." St. Paul uses it when he says, "For I received from the Lord what I also delivered to you" (1 Corinthians 11:23). The New Testament community was convinced of the possibility of handing over the goods, that some things could be committed, transmitted. At first this was done by oral tradition but at a very early time they also turned to written statements. Certain terms were used to indicate this type of material: *faith* (1 Timothy 3:13, 6:21, Jude 3); *confession* (1 Timothy 6:12, Hebrews 3:1, 10:23); *doctrine of Christ* (2 John 9); standard of teaching (Romans 6:17). The early Christians were convinced that there was a kernel of doctrine, which was normative and which could be expressed and passed on as a part of the living tradition of the community. These little confessional nuggets are usually found in the midst of statements of praise and also of recognition of sin. Confession of sin is a part of doxology because it is an acknowledgment of one's place before God, and thus is a statement of honor and praise to God for his mercy.

Another feature of life in the early church indicates this combination of confession of faith and doxology. The early Christians were marked off from contemporary Judaism by the confession, "Jesus is Messiah." In contrast to those who still waited for God to come and restore what was lost, some Christians affirmed that he had already and in fact done his great work in the person of Jesus of Nazareth. In the Roman world, however, another confession was needed. Here the words change to "Jesus [or Christ] is Lord." This was in direct opposition to the civil religion of that day which insisted that Caesar was Lord. The Christian confession was the cause for death in many instances. It praised God in the person of his son, and thus was a statement both of faith and of doxology. It was and is a part of the living tradition of the church.

Finally, consider the Confessions as *anchors*. In a time of theological and political relativism, when any position seems as acceptable as any other, as long as someone happens to feel strongly enough about it, the words of our Lord take on particular meaning, "Everyone then who hears these words of mine and does them will be like the wise man who built his house upon the rock (Matthew 7:24). Now, of course we cannot apply these words directly to the Confessions, but insofar as and because they present the Scriptures they are anchors.

Confessional statements are necessary. They are needed in connection with the unity of the church, to preserve the truth of the Scriptures, to guard the proclamation, to regulate life and teaching. Remember how they come from times of great stress and controversy. We will see how they addressed the issues and so held the community close to its central message.

Statements of faith are necessary. They are also very dangerous if they lead us to conclude that our correct words and statements somehow or other capture God and enable us to manipulate him to our own theological ends. If they hinder us from distinguishing between the Scriptures and the theological statements drawn from them, they are being used contrary to the intention of their writers. While they quote the church fathers, they note pointedly that the final test is always the Scriptures. The fathers of the church "were men who could err and be deceived" (Apol. XXIV, 95, p. 267).

For all of the dangers, such statements are necessary. We are not allowed the luxury of retreat into either mysticism or irrationalism. God addresses persons in his Word; he addresses the whole person, including the mind. Words, statements, intellect . . . all are to be used, but always with the note of humility, with a spirit of tentativeness that recognizes that our best statements are never the last word; that they are subject to error and are in need of constant correction; that we do see as through a mirror dimly (1 Corinthians 13:12); and that only in the final time will God make all things new and complete.

As an anchor the Confessions also are needed as a constant test of how we proclaim and live the message of our Lord. They serve as a guide to the interpretation of the Scriptures. Both the Scriptures and the Confessions hold the saving action of God in Jesus Christ as their central interpretive theme. When looking at the Word of God, the Lutherans underline the words, "these are written that you may believe that Jesus is the Christ,

the Son of God, and that believing you may have life
in his name" (John 20:31) .   •

The Lutheran documents center on Christ and the
event of salvation. This is the main message of the Scriptures and also provides the basic line of proper interpretation. "It leads in a preeminent way to the clear and
proper understanding of all of Scripture, it alone points
the way to the inexpressible treasure and right knowledge of Christ, and it alone opens the door into the
whole Bible. Without this article no poor conscience
can have a proper, constant, and certain comfort or dis-
cern the riches of Christ's grace" (Apol. IV, 2, p. 107).

Christ and his saving work on our behalf are the center
of the Scriptures; to confront us with this message is its
saving purpose. This message, this interpretation, is not
generally acceptable or popular; the gospel is always of-
fensive. The Confessions as anchor tend to pull us back
and hold us to the gospel center of the Christian message.

Finally, the Confessions serve as an anchor that holds
us from drifting into heresy. Heresy is a bad word for
some people today. The idea that someone can judge
another's position and declare it in error goes against
our commitment to freedom of expression, to pluralism
in thought and practice. However out of date it may
seem, the Confessors maintain that it is possible to de-
part from the apostolic faith, that it is possible to with-
draw from the faithful community. Certainly variety of
theological position is possible, even within the biblical
record. Certainly there are many voices claiming my attention, offering the latest insights into every possible
subject. But don't say they are all of equal value; don't
pretend they are all right, all acceptable as long as someone feels strongly about them and is committed to them.
It is possible to be wrong. And to be wrong in one's

relationship to God in Jesus Christ is a matter of permanent consequence.

By centering our thoughts on Jesus Christ, by calling us back again and again to this center, the Confessions provide a footing against the currents, winds, and tides that swirl around and within every believer.

How should we regard the Confessions today? As pointers, treasures, and anchors. As such they provide both continuity with the wealth of the insight of the past, and also openness and responsiveness to the needs of the present and future. On the basic issues they do address our day. They are and can be our confessions.

What does it mean to subscribe to the Confessions, to make them our own? It means to recognize that their contents are confession of faith, not rules; they are evangelical witnesses, not legal requirements. Therefore one does not witness *to*, but *with* the Confessions, as they and we subordinate ourselves to the Scriptures which point to the center, to Christ.

In this sense the Confessions are liberating documents because they constantly refer us to the gospel and tell us its meaning. They thus free us from all kinds of *autonomous* or *heteronomous* theologies; they free us to assume a *theonomous* stance. An autonomous theology centers upon, and takes direction from the self. One that is heteronomous is influenced by external forces. A theonomous stance sees all of life in relation to God.

The gospel, the good news of God in Jesus Christ, is always contrary to our natural schemes. We are by nature legalists, and would like to believe that in some way we have a claim on God, that his grace in some sense depends on our goodness, our intellect, our piety. The good news is that we are loved because of what God is, not what we are and deserve. This message is never something that one memorizes, or captures and then has forever. We are reminded of it each day, or we turn again to some self-centered, self-praising scheme, some theology of barter in which we trade our supposed goodness for God's approval and acceptance.

The gospel frees us, and the Confessions understand and lead us to the gospel. They may use language at times that is foreign to us and difficult to understand. They may fight some battles that no longer excite or interest us. They may even make historical and exegetical judgments that are incorrect. But they do direct us to the gospel, and so are freeing and enabling documents.

3   Justification: The Center of the Lutheran Confessions

Do you recall the outline for our study that was suggested earlier? It looked like this:

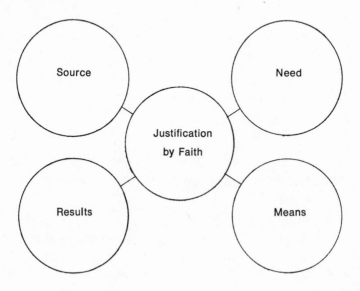

The readings in the Lutheran Confessions that refer most directly to our topic in this chapter might be placed in our center circle:

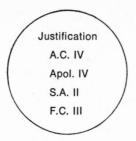

Justification
A.C. IV
Apol. IV
S.A. II
F.C. III

We are not starting at the beginning and treating the articles in some sort of structural order. Instead we are looking first at the center of the Lutheran affirmation. The significance of this emphasis on the work of Christ and how a relationship with God is established is clear in Luther's comment,

> Nothing in this article can be given up or compromised, even if heaven and earth and all things temporal should be destroyed. For as St. Peter says, there is no other name under heaven given among men by which we may be saved, and with his stripes we are healed. On this article rests all that we teach and practice. . . . Therefore we must be quite certain and have no doubts about it, otherwise, all is lost and our adversaries will gain the victory (S.A.II, i., p. 292) .

The authors of the Formula of Concord agree with this estimation:

> This article of justification by faith is "the chief article of the entire Christian doctrine," "without which no poor conscience can have any abiding comfort, or, rightly understand the riches of the grace of Christ."

In the same vein Dr. Luther declared, "Where this single article remains pure, Christendom will remain pure, in beautiful harmony, without any schisms; but where it does not remain pure, it is impossible to repel any error or heretical spirit" (F.C.S.D. III, p. 540).

It is possible to find the center of one's theological concern in some other place. Today, for example, some are trying to correct what seems to them to be an over-concentration on the Second Article of the Creed by emphasizing the work of God in creating and sustaining the world. Others are increasingly interested in the work of the Holy Spirit and find their moorings in the Third Article. Concentration on only one aspect of God's self-revelation to the exclusion of others is certainly not desirable.

There is no question about where the Lutheran writers have placed their emphasis. While not excluding concern for the fullness of the message, they hold up God's work in the person of Jesus Christ as the center of their thought. The God who creates and sustains has revealed himself and his purpose in Jesus Christ, whose work on our behalf becomes our own through the ministry of the Holy Spirit. Relationship to God is to be reestablished. This can only come about through Jesus Christ.

Two Ways to Regard Mankind

From their perspective there are only two ways of looking at, evaluating, and considering mankind. We must be clear which of these two ways or methods is being used in each instance.

The first way of regarding mankind is *coram homini-bus,* "in the presence of other persons," "in the presence of man." An individual, for example, who believed that there was no God at all would look at other persons this way. There is no God to worry about, therefore conversation about him, concern for him, and evaluation that includes him is not appropriate.

Another individual who might hold to the classical Deist position that there is a God, but this figure created the world and has now, as it were, spun it off into space to run down on its own, would also tend to regard persons in this way. God exists, but doesn't care. In both of these positions mankind is itself the ultimate measure of all things.

A third variation of this approach might be found in those who assert that God does in fact exist, that he cares for us, but that he has left judgment and rule to his representatives, the church.

The tendency in each of these is to view mankind from below, or from the same level. Comparison is always with persons. We are all drawn to some variation of this manner of judgment because by its use we can always manage to look quite good. Quite frankly most of us are very willing to be evaluated on the basis of comparison with other persons. Do you accuse me of drinking too much? Well, maybe you're right, but look at my neighbor down the street. There's a real drinker; his home life is destroyed, family gone, can't hold a job. Look at *him!* Do you accuse me of being dishonest? Well, maybe I borrow a few things, but I've never robbed a bank or been involved in any major fraud like some I could name. If you are a legalist at heart, and I believe we all are, then you would like to be evaluated in terms of keeping a law in outward sense, and always compared with other people.

But there is another way of evaluating human beings, and that is *coram Deo,* "in the presence of God." This position argues that God exists, cares, rules, and judges, and a person is understood only as in God's presence. To be in this presence is at the same moment a time of judgment and of grace. Here one looks at mankind from above, and the comparison is not with other persons, but with God and his will and perfection. The concern of the Lutheran Confessions is always with persons *coram Deo*.

How the Relationship with God Is Established

A basic question for all those who hold that there is a God who cares, rules, and judges, a question that came to particular prominence in the debates of the sixteenth century, is, how does one attain to relationship with God? At the risk of oversimplification we note three major answers that have been suggested within the Christian community.

The first one is related to a British monk named Pelagius who died around A.D. 420. Basically optimistic about human capacity, this position maintains that relationship is established as the individual, moved by the free will and guided by God's law, follows the example provided by Jesus Christ. The chief effort, and therefore credit, belongs to the person. A key concept in this scheme is that God would not have commanded what man is unable to perform. We can do something if we know that we ought to do it. God's grace in this view includes a person's free will, the sending of Christ as an example, and the giving of the law as a guide to conduct.

A second position, current in Luther's day and in our own, sees God's grace as a power which is infused into the person and which enables a certain effort or work. Relationship with God is established by a process, or, as Bonaventura, a prominent theologian in the Middle

Ages, put it, by "an ascent of the soul." The individual is not capable alone of establishing a tie to Deity, but God comes with prevenient grace, and the person, by virtue of innate capacities left over from the Fall, responds, doing what it is fitting. He thus acquires what is called a "merit of fittingness." God in turn responds to this with more grace, including love. The person acquires a certain disposition and responds further by good works until finally one acquires what is called a "merit of worthiness," a merit of justification. This position is sometimes called semi-Augustinianism. If the first position emphasizes the activity and credit of mankind, the second stresses shared activity and credit. This cooperative effort is sometimes termed *synergism*.

The great opponent of Pelagius was the theologian and bishop, Augustine. His path to becoming a Christian was long, bitter, full of torment and anguish. The reality and power of evil were a part of his experience, as were his complete inability and state of being lost apart from Christ. The writings of Scripture, especially St. Paul, filtered through his own experience, led Augustine to argue for the *monergism of grace*. If there is to be relationship it is due to the sole, powerful, gracious working of God—alone. Not man alone, prompted by a good example, not God and man cooperating in some way, but God alone. For better or worse, this is where the Reformers of the sixteenth century stood.

Luther's experience was one of absolute despair as he sought to find a merciful God by doing what lay within him, thus following the dictates of his teachers. His discovery of what relationship meant and how it was attained came as he studied the Scriptures, notably the concept of the righteousness of God in Psalms 31 and 71 and in Romans 1:16-17. He discovered that the righteousness of God is not some standard of perfection that

God demands of me, but rather it is something which God gives to those in faith. The direction of movement in establishing contact with God is one way only—from the top down. It is not caused by what I am and can contribute, but solely by what God is and intends for me. All other human religious schemes are based on the notion that God does business with *good* people. They may not be perfect, but they have done their best and God responds. Contrary to all this, the basic insight of the Reformation is that God does business with sinners. We are accepted, not because of our goodness, our wit, our beauty, but only because of his graciousness, his love, and his mercy.

Justification and Its Synonyms

When Lutherans have spoken about God's gracious dealing with sinners, they usually have used the words *justification by faith*. This expression itself causes some problems today, even for many Christians. It is possible that this formulation may not be the best way of expressing the fact for all people. At a recent meeting of the Lutheran World Federation, for example, some persons argued that there were better ways of talking about God's activity and his means of establishing relationship. The concept of justification, so prominent in St. Paul, involves a particular understanding of the human condition and of God. The word has legal connotations: the scene is the courtroom; God is the judge; man is the accused and is guilty. In this situation one person and one act frees the accused and guilty.

But how can we address persons who have a different concept of God and a varying awareness of sin and its effects? Is it necessary to convert them into first- or sixteenth-century people before we can speak of God's love and desire for them? Are there not other biblical pictures that are more useful in some instances today?

Most Lutherans still find the concept of justification by grace through faith congenial to their understanding. It is biblical and confessional; we do not need to replace it with another formulation. The question at this point is whether one can speak in different ways and still find a place within the boundaries afforded by the confessional stance. Several definitions or descriptions of God's act of establishing relationship are found within the Confessions. The most prominent is justification, but others are to be noted:

1. *Forgiveness of sins.* "But that we receive forgiveness of sins and become righteous before God by grace" (A.C. IV, p. 30. "Forgiveness of sins is the same as justification according to Psalm 32:1, 'Blessed is he whose transgression is forgiven'" (Apol. IV, p. 117).

2. *Absolution.* "Justified means in this article 'to absolve,' that is, to pronounce free from sin" (F.C.Ep. III, p. 473).

3. *Adoption.* "That the poor sinner is justified before God, that he is absolved and declared free from his sins . . . and he is adopted as a child of God, an heir of eternal life" (F.C.S.D. III, p. 540).

4. *Righteousness.* Justification "is to be pronounced or accounted righteous" (Apol. IV, p. 117) or "righteous before God by grace" (A.C. IV, p. 30).

5. *Reconciliation.* Many persons today find reconciliation a more meaningful concept than any other. They may not recognize or experience what the Scriptures describe as *guilt* in relation to sin, but they are often aware that things are not right between them and other people. There is an overriding feeling of aliena-

tion; we are separated from one another, and from
God, and even divided within ourselves. What can
the gospel say to this situation? In 2 Corinthians
there is an extended discussion which describes God's
work and ours in terms of reconciliation: "In Christ
God was reconciling the world to himself, . . . en-
trusting to us the message of reconciliation" (2 Cor.
5:19).

This theme is picked up by the Lutheran Confessions
where it is made parallel to forgiveness of sins, the
promise, God's favorable disposition, and justification
(Apol. IV, pp. 112-113).

Declaration or Inner Change?

All of these ways of speaking, *justification, forgiveness,
absolution, adoption, righteousness,* and *reconciliation*
refer to a judgment that has been made by God, to a
relationship that has been established by a declarative
act of God. One is declared justified, reconciled, adopted,
or forgiven. This is the biblical view, because the words
for *righteousness* in both Old and New Testaments refer
primarily to a declaration of judgment.[1]

A key word in the Pauline presentation is *reckoning*
or *accounting.* This is a bookkeeping term. Something
is taken from one ledger to another. When the Reformers speak of reckoning they do it in two ways: first, there
is a non-reckoning of sin, and second, a reckoning, or
accounting of the righteousness of Christ to the believer.
Sin is not reckoned, while what Christ has done on behalf of the believer is. Abraham believed God, and it
was reckoned to him as righteousness (Romans 4:3). God
looks at those who are in Christ, according to the Confessors, as though they had never sinned.

The main emphasis in the Confessions is on the declarative, forensic act of God in establishing our righteousness. They always wish to speak of Christ's righteousness, something which comes from outside of us, as being reckoned or counted to us. One of the controversies which led to the Formula of Concord was caused by a theologian who maintained that the believer comes to have an essential righteousness of his own, and on this basis God accepts him. The negative response of the Confessors to this suggestion was overwhelming. At the same time another theme is occasionally heard, one that has caused debate among Lutherans. Both themes are found in one sentence.

> Regarding faith, we maintain that because of Christ by faith itself, we are truly accounted righteous and accepted before God [the declarative emphasis], and to be justified means to make unrighteous men righteous, or to regenerate them as well as to be pronounced or accounted righteous. For Scripture speaks both ways. (Apol. IV, p. 117).

Are they speaking simply of a declaration or also of an inner change? The same question can be found in Luther. While the emphasis on the declarative is overwhelming, at the same time Luther can speak of being justified "more and more," and frequently uses the image of the physician in describing the work of Christ. There is movement, development, and process, not simply a declared act by a force external to the self.

The same type of tension between a declaration or an inner change is found in the statement, "It is indeed correct to say that believers who through faith in Christ have been justified, possess in this life first the reckoned righteousness of faith, and second also the inchoate righteousness of the new obedience, or of good works" (F.C.S.D. III, p. 544).

What is it, declaration, or inner change and movement? The Lutheran Confessions say *both*, with a heavy emphasis on declaration. Viewed from the perspective of God's promise and saving activity—seen from above, if you will—all is complete, we have been declared righteous, we are in fellowship. From the perspective of our own experience, however, we recognize the continued struggle with evil, the reality of change and movement in the relationship.

In all of this discussion there is a great concern that no one confuse the establishment of relationship with what follows after it, that is, with sanctification or the Christian life.

Remember how the Confessions spoke of the inchoate righteousness? The word *inchoate* means *unformed, incipient.*

> But because the inchoate renewal remains imperfect in this life, and because sin dwells in the flesh, even in the regenerated, righteousness of faith before God can be produced solely in the gracious reckoning of Christ's righteousness to us, without the addition of our works, so that our sins are forgiven and covered up and are not reckoned to our account. Here, too, if the article of justification is to remain pure, we must give special diligent heed that we do not mingle or insert that which precedes faith or follows faith in the article of justification (F.C.S.D. III, p. 543).

The concern is not so much with our experience, but with how we stand *coram Deo*, "in the presence of God." There is only one thing that can enable us to stand there.

The two kinds of righteousness, declared and inner-inchoate, "dare not be confused with one another or introduced simultaneously into the article of justification by faith before God, for because this inchoate righteousness or renewal in us is imperfect and impure in this life, on account of the flesh, no one can therewith and thereby stand before the Tribunal of God" (F.C.S.D. III, p. 545).

Only the righteousness of the obedience, passion and death of Christ which is reckoned to the believer through faith can stand before God. Hence even after renewal, after one has lived in the new obedience, still one is pleasing, acceptable, adopted only on account of Christ. Everything is by God's gracious action. There is never a moment in life when he owes us anything because of what we have done or are.

Justification in Outline

The most pointed, brief and clear summary of what we wish to say is found in the Fourth Article of the Augsburg Confession. This may be outlined as follows:

A. *The impossibility of self-justification in the presence of God*
   1. The errors of the opponents
   2. Justification, not by our strengths, merits, or works

B. *God justifies*
   1. Freely
   2. Because of Christ
   3. Through faith

The context of this statement is the controversy in which the writers were engaged. On the one hand they faced certain of the left wing of the Reformation who maintained that relationship with God was established and maintained by means of perfect discipleship. They emphasized discipleship, reality in the Christian life, and martyrdom. Many of them had a rather optimistic view of human capacity to do good before God. On the other hand, the Reformers were opposed to what they understood to be a Roman Catholic position, which stressed some sort of co-working with God, some co-operative effort to effect fellowship.

Both of these positions shared, in varying degrees, certain basic misconceptions, according to the Confessions. First, they had an overly optimistic view of mankind and its capacity to cooperate in establishing fellowship with God. As we will see the Lutherans are very pessimistic about human capacity "in the presence of God."

In the second instance the opponents are in error because they have misunderstood the law of God, seeing it as a means of salvation and seeing Christ as a new lawgiver. Luther himself, in certain early writings, had spoken of Christ as bringing a new law, but in his mature theology insisted that "Christ is not another Moses."

Melanchthon developed this theme:

> We see that there are books in existence which compare certain teachings of Christ with the teachings of Socrates, Zeno, and others as though Christ had come to give some sort of laws by which we could merit the forgiveness of sins rather than receive it freely for his merits. So if we accept this teaching of the opponents, that we merit forgiveness of sins and justification by the works of reason, there will be no difference between philosophical or Pharisaic righteousness and Christian righteousness (Apol. IV, p. 109).

Philosophical or civil righteousness has its place and is to be praised, *coram hominibus,* "in the presence of men," but "in the presence of God" it is of no avail. And so the Lutherans insisted that their opponents were wrong about the purpose of the law, and on Christ's work. The purpose of the law of God is to drive us to Christ, who is not a new lawgiver, but the savior.

The third fault of the opponents was that they not only misunderstood the law but also emphasized the wrong part of it. By tradition the Ten Commandments had been divided into two tables. The first dealt with our relation to God, the second with our relations with our fellows. By concentrating on the second the central issue is avoided.

Although it is somewhat possible to do civil works, that is, the outward works of the law, without Christ and the Holy Spirit, still the impulses of the heart toward God, belonging to the essence of the divine law, are impossible without the Holy Spirit. This is evident from what we have already said. Our opponents are fine theologians, they look at the second table and political works. About the first table they care nothing, as though it were irrelevant, or at best they require only outward acts of worship. They utterly overlook that eternal law far beyond the sense and understanding of all creatures: "You shall love the Lord your God with all your heart" (Apol. IV, p. 125).

Once again, the issue is, where are you standing? In whose presence are you evaluating yourself and others? If you wish to concentrate on man in the presence of other men then the use of the second table is satisfactory and natural. Here is something you can get your teeth into, something to put your hands on. I can make some judgment whether I am, in fact, an adulterer, or robber, or murderer. These are all significant judgments, and necessary ones in civil society, but the crucial issue at this point is, "How do you stand in the presence of

God?" For this only the first table is sufficient as a basis of judgment.

The conclusion of all this is that it is not possible to justify oneself before God by one's own strength, merits, or works (A.C. IV, p. 30). We cannot, by our own reason or strength believe in Jesus Christ or come to him (S.C. p. 345).

> Accordingly we believe, teach, and confess that our righteousness before God consists in this, that God forgives us our sins purely by his grace, without any preceding, present, or subsequent work, merit, or worthiness and reckons to us the righteousness of Christ's obedience, on account of which righteousness we are accepted by God into grace and regarded as righteous (F.C.Ep. III, 2, p. 473).

God justifies, freely, because of Christ through faith. This is a sentence to remember and to hold fast. *God justifies freely, by grace.* Here grace is not conceived as some sort of infused power which enables me to do God-pleasing work and thus be acceptable.[2] It is not a substance or stuff that is dispensed by the church through the sacraments, and which may also be withheld by the church. Grace is essentially an attitude *within God.* It is his disposition of benevolence, of kindness toward sinners. It is the favor of God.

Justification is a gift. The witness of St. Paul looms large in this understanding. "Being justified freely by his grace through the redemption that is in Christ" (Romans 3:24).

> But the free gift is not like the trespass . . . the free gift in the grace of that one man Jesus Christ abounded for many. And the free gift is not like the effect of that one man's sin . . . but the free gift following

many trespasses brings justification . . . much more will those who receive the abundance of grace and the free gift of righteousness reign in life through the one man Jesus Christ (Romans 5:17-19).

"For by grace you have been saved through faith; and this is not your own doing, it is the gift of God—not because of works, lest any man should boast" (Eph. 2:8).

This is the first thing to say: that God justifies freely, by grace. Whatever synonym you want to use, whatever picture you want to paint, the center of it must always be God's grace, and freedom, and gift.

God justifies freely, *because of Christ,* or for Christ's sake. If we cannot be reconciled, adopted, forgiven, justified because of our own efforts and capabilities, there must be some other basis for fellowship with God. It comes because of Christ.

Therefore the righteousness which by grace is reckoned to faith or to the believers is the obedience, the passion, and the resurrection of Christ when he satisfied the law for us and paid for our sin. Since Christ is not only man, but God and man, one undivided person, he was as little under the law—since he is the Lord of the law—as he was obligated to suffer and die for his person. Therefore his obedience consists not only in his suffering and dying, but also in his spontaneous subjection to the law in our stead and his keeping of the law in so perfect a fashion that, reckoning it to us as righteousness, God forgives us our sins, accounts us holy and righteous, and saves us forever on account of this entire obedience which, by doing and suffering, in life and in death, Christ rendered for us to his heavenly Father (F.C.S.D. III, p. 541).

It is the work of the whole Christ, divine and human,

who was obedient "even unto death on the cross" (Phil.
2:8) that provides the basis for our new life. Our sins
are not reckoned, while his righteousness is. The believer
is still a sinner; life is still a struggle; but in all things
God looks on the believer as though he had never sinned.
The sinner is counted as righteous because of Christ.
This is the basis for Luther's repeated saying that the
believer is "at the same time sinner and justified," or his
description of the Christian as "always sinner, always
penitent, always justified." [3]

The obedience of Christ, to which the Reformers return again and again, is described in two ways. His *active*
obedience consists in his fulfilling of the law, although
he was himself lord of the law. His *passive* obedience
is found in his suffering innocently and dying for us.
It is the whole life of the whole Christ that is involved
in our relationship with God.

Many different theories have been constructed over
the centuries to describe Christ's atoning work. Each of
the major views has some biblical roots; each is also
a product of its historical context. Lutherans hold a place
for all of them, although the theme that emphasizes
Christ's victorious struggle over evil is dominant.[4]

At times there are references to Christ's offering or being a ransom, or of his being a satisfaction which restored
God's honor, or of his being an example of divine love
which transforms those who see it. Any position is only
a halting attempt to describe something that defies explanation; and other themes or pictures are necessary
for a more complete picture. Whichever view is most
congenial to you, the confessional stance is that the actor,
the doer is God, and what he has done in Jesus Christ
is the basis for our relationship. God justifies freely, because of, on account of, Christ.

God justifies freely, because of Christ, *through faith.*

God saving work in Christ comes to us and becomes ours through faith. This is the instrument by which relationship is effected.

It is important at the outset of this discussion to make a distinction. One is accepted *through* faith, not *because of,* or *after* faith. The difference is crucial, for if I maintain that I am justified *because of* faith, then faith becomes a meritorious act or virtue by means of which I have a claim on God. But I never have a claim on him; his attitude and effort toward me are based on nothing but sheer grace and mercy.

The saving aspect of faith is its object, that to which it lays hold, to the promise of God in Jesus Christ. "For faith does not justify because it is so good a work and so God-pleasing a virtue, but because it lays hold on and accepts the merits of Christ and the promise of the holy gospel" (F.C.S.D. III, p. 541).

Faith refers exclusively to the promise; "as an act of man it is altogether empty." [5]

The Tension Between Faith and Response

Christians, and Lutherans in particular, have always found themselves in tension when they think about the nature of faith. The problem is understanding it as both a gift of God, and the response of the person. The Confessors follow Luther in consistently emphasizing that faith itself is a gift from God, a work of the Holy Spirit. "But we are talking about a faith that is not an idle thought, but one that frees us from death, brings forth new life in our hearts, and is the work of the Holy Spirit" (Apol. IV, p. 116; cf. also S.C. p. 345). The ability to believe, to trust, is not innate; faith in God's promise is not self-generated, but is the result of the work of the Spirit.

On the other hand it is necessary to think of faith in terms of my response, a response which, if you will, allows God to do something, or which simply accepts what he wishes to do (Apol. IV, p. 114).

At times our inability to establish relationship is put in extreme terms. Persons apart from Christ and the work of the Spirit are described as being like logs, or rocks, or stones, unable to initiate action. They are even worse than these inanimate objects, for they are actually at enmity with God (F.C.S.D. II, p. 532).

On the other hand, I am not after all a log, rock, or stone, but a person, and God has chosen to deal with me as a person. No one else, however pious or well meaning, can believe for me, can accept the gift. It is possible *not* to be persuaded by the preaching of the gospel, the invitation to faith. Even if we speak of response, however, no one can remain within the boundaries of the Lutheran stance and maintain that such response is an act of obedience which causes God to respond or which places some claim upon him. One cannot respond without the work of the Holy Spirit who comes as a gracious gift (S.C. p. 345).

One finds this same tension present in Luther. When facing those who seemed to be claiming that their good works, including faith, were in some way affecting God, he consistently replied, "Faith is not a work; it is a gift of God." [6] On the other side, in the "Treatise on Good Works" he identifies faith as the chief of all good works.[7]

What kind of faith are they describing, this gift and response? It is not what some of their contemporaries described as "faith formed in love," which emphasized the loving activity which shaped faith. This was faith-plus. It is not a "historical faith," which is merely a knowledge of historical data. Nor is it a "general faith," which believes that there is a God who is powerful, but not necessarily concerned with me. No, it is a *fides Christi,* a faith which focuses and centers on the person and work of Christ. It is not sufficient, Luther argued, to believe that God is, that he has created and cares, or even that Jesus Christ lived and died and rose again. Rather Christ ought to be preached so that he becomes Christ *for you* and Christ *for me.*[8]

These little words, these little pronouns, "for you," "for us," are the most difficult in all of Scripture. It is one thing, for example, to believe that all persons are sinners. I can live with that, and even be comfortable with it. It is quite another to recognize that *I* am a sinner. So also it is one thing to believe that Christ died for the sins of the whole world. It is another thing when I suddenly realize that he died for *me.* It is all *for me,* and *for you.*

Faith was often considered by the Reformers from three angles. First, it includes knowledge of the facts and claims of the promises of God. On a second level, faith includes agreement that this is true. On the deepest level, it involves trust, personal commitment to the promise and the God who has made it. Faith trusts in the God who promises, even without proof—or in some instances in spite of the evidence. What Luther termed a "theology of glory" insisted on rational, empirical support for faith; a "theology of the cross," however, is content simply with the promise. God even hides himself, and still the promise holds. The repeated "no" of God, as to the Syrophoenician woman who persisted in petitioning Jesus (Mark 7:24-30) hides a deep and secret "yes" for those who cling to the promise. Men, Luther said, hide themselves in order to be hidden; God hides himself in order to be revealed.[9]

Faith, which is both gift and response, clings to the promise which is freely given but based on the work and person of Christ for me, and for us (Apol. IV, p. 114).

It is God who justifies, freely, because of Christ, through faith. Why have theologians spent so much time and ink on this simple sentence? Why are they so irritated with their opponents as to claim that they "understood neither the forgiveness of sins nor faith nor grace no righteousness and confuse this doctrine most miserably" (Apol. IV, p. 107)? Because of their conviction that the sentence is true to the biblical witness and the message of the gospel through the ages. If one is confused on this major point, two things happen. First, the glory and blessing of Christ are obscured. Second, pious consciences are robbed of the consolation offered them in Christ.

Christ's honor is obscured when we place ourselves beside him and claim to add to or complete what he has done for us. This is why the Confessors take pains to stress what they call the "exclusive terms": "apart from works, without the law, by grace, and through faith alone." I maintain this first insight is correct on the basis of the Scripture and the tradition of the church. The second insight, that pious consciences are robbed of their comfort by confusion on this matter, I maintain by experience. When one is drawn, however piously, to rely on good character, works, good deeds apart from, or in addition to the work of Christ, there is nothing of substance to grasp in time of trial and death. Only the promise of God that he is gracious to those who trust, however haltingly, in him is sufficient food for consolation and lasting hope.

God justifies freely because of Christ through faith.

4   The Source of Justification

As we move to the second part of our circular outline it will be advisable that we keep the diagram in mind and also attempt to maintain some sort of dialog between the two sections.

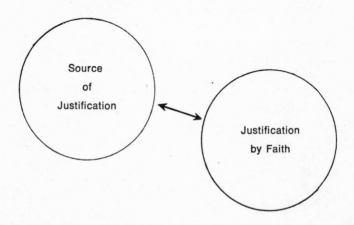

The reading which will enhance your understanding of this chapter is abbreviated in this circle.

Source of
Justification
A.C. I, III, XVII
Apol. I, III, XVII
S.C., L.C.—Creed
F.C. VIII, IX, XI
F.C. VIII, IX, XI

Speaking of God

From what has already been said, it should be evident that the new relationship cannot have the character or activities of humankind as its basis. It is God who justifies freely because of Christ, and through faith.

But what is God? Can even a tentative description or definition be offered? In the Large Catechism Luther asks, "What is it to have a God? What is God?" and answers, "A god is that to which we look for all good and in which we find refuge in every time of need. . . . That to which your heart clings and entrusts itself is, I say, really your God" (L.C. I, p. 365).

This statement allows room both for true worship and idolatry. It is as current as tomorrow's sunrise, for our own god is still in fact that from which we expect every good, to which we flee in need, to which our heart clings, and to which it entrusts itself. Money, power, position, economics, education: all can be god for us.

Or we can look to him whom we meet in Jesus Christ. This is the God about whom the Confessors wish to speak. The existence of God is a "given" for the writers. In the Augsburg Confession, Articles I and III, they do not argue, but simply accept the affirmations of the ecumenical creeds, concentrating on the unity of the work

of the Holy Trinity. Their Roman Catholic contemporaries accepted their statement and recognized it as orthodox. They make no attempt to demonstrate this by
logical argumentation. If you are looking through the
documents for help or support in how to argue the existence of God with a non-believer you will find no real
help. There is no concern for the type of debate so common to the Middle Ages. When the Confessors look to
Anselm it is to study his understanding of the work of
Christ, not to pick his arguments for God based on the
nature of the Deity or upon some notion of grades of
perfection. So also the famous five proofs cited by St.
Thomas Aquinas, based on the nature of the created
order, do not excite or interest them. In contrast to their
immediate theological forbears, the Lutheran Confessors
leap back over the centuries to the biblical understanding
of God as the "living God." They share with the writers
of the Scriptures a lack of interest in arguing for the
existence of God. They rather wish to describe, as they
understand it, the God who acts, who moves, who does
things—the God who is living. To suggest to an Old
Testament writer that he prove God's existence would
make about as much sense as demanding that I logically
demonstrate that my wife exists; and the answer would
be comparable: "I don't have to prove she exists; she
spoke to me this morning, and fed me. When I was ill
last week, she cared for me." Does God exist? The writer
of the Old Testament would respond, "He freed us from
slavery and led us through the wilderness to the land."
He is the living God.

This understanding pictures God as a dynamic being,
one of power and action, rather than as some sort of
static, unmoved first mover. It is a functional concept
concerned with what God does, rather than with the
questions of being. It is concerned with God's work

rather than with what it is that constitutes the deity. The interest is not with God's essence, but with his purpose; not what the deity is like in his interior workings, but with what he does in the world and in particular, in relation to mankind.

God and the World

If we are primarily concerned about God's relationship with the created order, rather than with God's nature, what options exist for describing the connection between God and the world? At the risk of oversimplification, let me suggest some of the ways in which this has been described over the centuries.

In the understanding of *pantheism,* God and the world are in some sense identified with one another. The notion of transcendence disappears in favor of a type of identification.

Another option is *monism* which insists that there is but one ultimate principle or material. If it is mind, the principle is *idealism;* if it is matter, it is *materialism;* or something that is neither mind nor matter may be the ground for both. When this picture is used as a description of God's relationship to the world, it is commonly asserted that the deity is the world's soul, and the cosmos, or created order, is his body. The point to note in both pantheism and monism is that there is no real, no essential difference between God and the world.

The very opposite of these schemes is *dualism.* Here one does not speak at all of dependence or identity. There are, rather, two eternal absolutes which stand in opposition. These may be conceived of in different ways: as light and darkness, as good and evil, or as matter (that which is worked upon to bring order from chaos) and spirit (the working factor).

Another option that also stresses no real connection, no dependence, is *deism*. God created once, but now the world is on its own, either running down or maintaining itself without the need of the deity.

A fifth option, one that predominates the Judeao-Christian understanding, sees God as *creator*. There are a number of important corollaries to this understanding. As creator, God is different from, and other than, the world. This affirmation stands in direct opposition to both pantheism and monism. As created matter, the world is not eternal. This understanding stands in opposition to all forms of absolute dualism. Finally, as created, the world always depends on God for sustenance. This stands in opposition to deism. The key words in this understanding of the created order, the cosmos, are difference, dependence, and interrelatedness. God and the world are different; the created order is continually dependent upon God; and there is constant interrelation between the two.

How Is God Known?

If God does exist and is related in some way to the creation, another important question follows: How can one know him, his works and his will? There are two major answers to this which are not necessarily mutually exclusive. They do, in fact, sometimes interpenetrate each other.

The first is sometimes called *natural theology*. In it the created order itself, including mankind, is the material for analysis, and from the analysis one draws certain conclusions about God. Lutherans have sometimes been overly antagonistic to this approach, partly in reaction to some of their contemporaries in the sixteenth century and earlier figures who placed great store by it. It is not proper to overreact to the point where it is maintained that nothing of God is to be seen in nature. St. Paul argues, "Ever since the creation of the world his invisible nature, namely, his eternal power and deity, has been clearly perceived in the things that have been made" (Romans 1:20).

The fact that knowledge gained in this way is inevitably used badly does not alter Paul's understanding that it does exist. The self-revelation of God in creation has led people to stress learning about God from this source. One concludes from nature and its workings that God is rational, powerful, and eternal, among other things. In addition, since mankind is a part of creation and is in "the image of God," (Genesis 1:27), it is possible to draw certain conclusions by analyzing man. If you take the good qualities in humans, and in a sense multiply them to infinity, you have some clues about God. On the other hand, the bad attributes of humanity are denied to God since he is perfect. These two methods are part of the so-called "analogy of being" and are known as the *via positiva* (positive way) and the *via negativa* (the negative way).

There are certain strengths in this approach. For one thing, it emphasizes God's gift of some knowledge to all persons, and it takes creation, with utmost seriousness. It also stresses that humans, even when separated from God, are still rational and inquiring beings. They have not ceased to be human by virtue of sin.

There are limitations, however, and here is where many of the Reformers have concentrated their attention. Knowledge of God attained in this way is inevitably turned to wrong ends. This is the argument which Paul uses in Romans 1.

Another limitation is that the picture of God taken from the analysis of creation alone is incorrect. One must be selective of what is analyzed, for example, to come to the conclusion that God is love. Only beautiful babies, glorious sunsets, waving fields of wheat, "Purple mountain majesties above the fruited plain," and the like will fit here. There is no way to account for the broader picture, which includes birth defects, famines, earthquakes, and floods. The picture of God one receives from nature, at the very best, is one of capriciousness—of great kindness at times, and also of terrible cruelty and wrath. This is most definitely a limitation on natural theology used alone.

If we base our understanding on the notion of the "image of God," we tend to create a god in our own image. If we believe our basic characteristics are, or should be, love and mercy, then our God must be all-loving and all merciful. The conclusion of this is universalism, the teaching that eventually all people will be saved. If the predominant feature in my personal makeup is the sexual urge and I am in the image of God, I can end up with a fertility cult and worship Baal or Ashtaroth, or their modern counterparts. If judgment is prominent in my makeup, then I can support the notion of *karma*. If I lean to a system of determinism, I can end up with a God that is equal to Fate. In each of these I end by worshiping a creature rather than the Creator (Romans 1:25). This is a subtle temptation. Some psychiatrists maintain that Christians are guilty of doing precisely this, of projecting their desires and insecurities on the screen of the universe and calling that "God."

A final limitation to this approach to the knowledge of God is that it tends to move into an area the Reformers called the *deus absconditus,* the hidden God. It attempts to pry out the secrets of God. The hiddenness of God is a basic concept for the Confessors. God's eternal nature, his plan and purpose have not been revealed to us. He works, as it were, behind masks in creation, in the orders of society, and even in the figure of Christ. God is not immediately perceived in the figure of Christ, but only to eyes of faith. His hiddenness is also evident in the fact that he works "under the sign of the opposite," in ways that are contrary to our reasonable expectations. He hides himself in order to be revealed to the eyes of faith.

In summary we might note that the Lutherans wish to say that mankind does have a "dim spark of the knowledge that there is a God" (S.D. II, 9, p. 521), but this is only an indefinite and general knowledge and when used, when turned into ritual it results only in idolatry.

> Thus natural man knows that there is a God, but not who God is, and so he does not know God the Creator. He knows in part what is demanded, but not who demands it, and therefore he does not recognize God's wrath. He knows neither God, nor his own reality; the innate internal uncleanness of human nature is not seen by him, and "this cannot be adjudged except from the Word of God." [1]

Luther puts it another way: "Although the whole world has sought painstakingly to learn what God is and what he thinks and does, yet it has never succeeded in the least" (L.C., p. 419). In short, natural theology can indicate God as lawgiver, judge and Creator, but the knowledge is neither clear, nor certain, and it is always perverted.

The Center Is Christ

How does one know God? Not by natural theology alone, but by revelation. Not by looking at and probing into the *deus absconditus,* but by clinging to the *deus revelatus,* "the God who has revealed himself." One knows God through the self-disclosure of a person and his will, and this only in Jesus Christ. This does not limit theology to discussion of the Second Article of the Creed, as Lutherans are accused of doing, but provides the focus, the basis for seeing the whole of God's activity.

In Jesus Christ God is seen as Creator and as Father of Christ and of all believers. In Christ the creation reveals God as the father who originates, purposes, and sustains. Luther puts it:

> I believe that God has created me and all that exists; that he has given me and still sustains my body and soul, all my limbs and senses, my reason and all the faculties of my mind, together with food and clothing, house and home, family and property; that he provides me daily and abundantly with all the necessities of life, protects from all danger, and preserves me from all evil. All this he does out of his pure, fatherly, and divine goodness and mercy, without any merit or worthiness on my part (S.C., p. 345).

God has created, and continues to sustain, that I might have fellowship with him. He sustains now by grace on the one hand, and by law and the structures of society on the other. He has not left the world to run its own particular way independently, but rules and sustains there also.

In Christ the Scripture reveals God and his purpose. The themes of Exodus, the chosen people, promise and restoration, fulfillment in Christ, and the hope of a future completeness are played and replayed in hundreds of ways by the Confessors. It is in the Word of God, seen as Christ himself, as the Scripture, and as oral proclamation of the message, that God reveals himself and his purpose for us (A.C. III, p. 29; Apol. Preface, 9, p. 99; A.C. XXVIII, 49, p. 89; Apol. IV, 108, p. 122;

L.C. II, 38, p. 415; L.C. II, 52, p. 417; L.C. V, 31, p. 450; F.C. Ep. II, 13, p. 471; F.C.S.D. II, 50, 52, pp. 530, 531).

The Catechisms in particular place great emphasis on creation, not only on who has done and is doing it, and that it is done by grace, but also on its significance for the individual. "We should emphasize," Luther insists, "the words, 'maker of heaven and earth.' " "What," he asks, "is meant by these words, 'I believe in God the Father Almighty, Maker of heaven and earth'?"

> Answer: I hold and believe that I am a creature of God; that is, that he has given and constantly sustains my body, soul, and life, my members great and small, all the faculties of my mind, my reason and understanding, and so forth; my food and drink, clothing, means of support, wife and child, servants, house and home, etc. Besides, he makes all creation help provide the comforts and necessities of life—sun, moon and stars in the heavens, day and night, air, fire, water, the earth and all that it brings forth, birds and fish, beasts, grain and all kinds of produce. Moreover, he gives all physical and temporal blessings—good government, peace, security. Thus we learn from this article that none of us has his life of himself, or anything else that has been mentioned here or can be mentioned, nor can he by himself preserve any of them, however small and unimportant (L.C., p. 412).

Finally, in Christ, the Holy Spirit reveals God as Father, creator, sustainer. We will return to what the documents wish to affirm about the Holy Spirit in a moment.

It is in Jesus Christ that God reveals himself to and for us (A.C., III: Apol. III; F.C. VIII). Not only has the Father-Creator provided us with life and all we need, great gifts all of them, but he has done something more.

Looking at the Second Article of the Creed, Luther exclaims, "Here we learn to know the second person of the
Godhead, and we see that we receive from God over and
above the temporal good mentioned above—that is, how
he has completely given himself to us, withholding nothing" L.C. p. 413). This understanding that in Christ we
meet God who has *given himself to us, withholding nothing,* is what causes Luther to stand in such awe before
Christ. We are not viewing a great man, a prophet, a
representative, an angel in Jesus Christ, but rather God.
Luther's conviction of this was unshakable.

In response to the question, "Who is Jesus Christ?" the
Confessors, as noted earlier, are in the tradition of the
ancient church. When the Roman Catholic theologians
responded to the Augsburg Confession they found no
fault with its christological affirmations. The answer to
the identity question as it relates to Christ is in two
parts: He is truly God and truly human. The documents
cite with approval various texts which assert his pre-
existence (John 1:1-3), that the world was created through
him (Hebrews 1:1-3), that all things were made through
him (Col. 1:15), that he enjoyed a unique relationship
with his Father (Phil. 2:5-11), and his own testimony to
himself (John 17:5, 18, 24).

The emphasis on the incarnation, his being "made
flesh" is also noted in the Gospels (e.g., John 1:14).

The Lutheran Confessions show a major concern for
Christ's function, for the work that he has done and
continues to do on our behalf. This emphasis is in keeping with the concept of the "living God" mentioned
earlier. Everything is to be seen in this light, even when
it seems that a concern for the nature and inner workings of Christ takes center stage.

This happens in Article VIII of the Formula of Concord in a discussion of the two natures of Christ. There

the opponents, ancient and modern, are identified: Nestorius, Eutyches, Arius, the Docetists, even Zwingli and Calvin. The concern is not for the nature of Christ or the psychology of Jesus, but for the reality of his saving work, and for the reality of his presence for us in the Lord's Supper.

Article VII of the Formula deals with the Sacrament of the Altar and asks how it is possible for us to affirm the presence of Christ in the Sacrament. Is it not true, as the Zwinglians would say, that because he has assumed human nature, he is now limited in space to the right hand of the Father? How can he be there and in all these places at the same time? Luther would respond that a more adequate Christology would recognize that the risen Christ, the glorified Christ, though fully human, shares completely in the various attributes of the Father. It is therefore proper to assert that he is everywhere present. The whole discussion about the sharing of attributes in the divine-human Christ is meant to speak to the issues of the reality of his work for us, both in the incarnation and in the Supper which is, in a sense, an extension of the incarnation. God showed that he meant business in his purpose, his promise to save, by the reality of the incarnation. Christ's presence in the Supper in this context, is an indication that his promise is to be believed, that he is still active and present.

Is not all this talk about the divine and human in Christ a type of theological game-playing that is best relegated to esoteric classes at seminaries, a historical relic that need not concern us today? Not unless one wishes to lose the heart of the Christian message. The humanity of Christ, for example, is a guarantee of the realism of God's work on our behalf. His love has come near to us, not simply as a verbal promise, but in the flesh of a person, like us (Hebrews 2:18; 4:15).

What about the divinity of Christ? Is he a great teacher, an example, a perfect model, an ideal to be emulated?
Is he a supreme religious genius, the greatest of the
prophets who leads us back to eternal religious truths?
An emphasis on the divinity of Christ argues that he is
not just teacher, example, perfect ideal, supreme religious genius, or prophet; he is God himself, from whom
there is no appeal, and beyond whom there is no need.
To lessen this is to deny the finality and assurance which
the Scriptures ascribe to him. The divinity of Christ is the
assurance of the authority of his proclamation and promise. It is to be understood in terms of Immanuel, "God
with us," God himself come near to us, in our midst
(Isaiah 7:14; Matthew 1:23) .

Finally, an affirmation of unity of the divine and human in the one Christ is assurance of the contemporan-
eity of the gospel; Christ is present today in the unity of
his person to accomplish his work among us. This is the
point of Luther's insistence that he who meets us in
Word and Sacrament is the whole Christ in his divine
humanity.

In the New Testament the work of Christ is pictured
in different ways depending on how the condition of
mankind is described. If man's condition is described in
terms of guilt, Christ's work is seen in sacrificial terms,
and results in the removal of guilt. If man is seen as
slave to sin and evil, Christ's efforts are cast in terms of
combat and victory, which results in freedom. If mankind is seen as enemy of God, Christ is seen as the recon-
ciler who breaks down walls and draws the opponents
into reconciliation.

The Confessors pick up these themes and use them in
various ways. Luther, for example, cites Romans, Isaiah,
and John, when he comments,

The first and chief article is this, that Jesus Christ, our God and Lord, "was put to death for our trespasses and raised again for our justification." He alone is "the lamb of God, who takes away the sin of the world." "God has laid on him the iniquities of us all." Moreover, "all have sinned," and "they are justified by his grace as a gift, through the redemption which is in Christ Jesus, by his blood." All of this comprises the "chief article" which cannot be given up or compromised (S.A. III, p. 292) .

Words that are more familiar to many are used in the Small Catechism, in the explanation of the Second Article.

I believe that Jesus Christ, true God, begotten of the Father from eternity, and also true man, born of the virgin Mary, is my Lord, who has redeemed me, a lost and condemned creature, delivered me and freed me from all sins, from death, and from the power of the devil, not with silver and gold but with his holy and precious blood and with his innocent sufferings and death, in order that I may be his, live under him in his kingdom, and serve him in everlasting righteousness, innocence, and blessedness, even as he is risen from the dead and lives and reigns to all eternity. This is most certainly true (S.C. p. 345) .

In describing the work of Christ, the writers find certain pictures helpful. Christ is God in action This follows from Luther's conviction that in Christ, God has given himself totally to us. In this person we see the God who would otherwise remain in darkness. "As we explained before, we could never come to recognize the Father's favor and grace were it not for the Lord Christ, who is a mirror of the Father's heart. Apart from him we see nothing but an angry and terrible Judge" (L.C., p. 419).

Another picture is Christ as an example or model. While some Lutherans and other Protestants are uncomfortable about speaking of Christ as model, since there is always a danger that imitation may lead to works righteousness, it is nevertheless a helpful concept and can be handled responsibly. To say that Christ is example or model would be to say that he is man as God intended. He is the man "for others," open to the world. He is self-giving instead of being curved to the earth or curved within one's self (classical ways of describing sin). He is open to the world, to God, and to other people.

Another descriptive word the Confessors apply to Christ is *exemplar*. He shows God's way of dealing with all persons. Just as God crushed Jesus in order to raise him up, so he deals with us, specifically through the law and the gospel.

The picture that dominates the entire discussion, however, is that of Savior, i.e., Redeemer and Lord. He is Savior, not only from original sin as the Catholic contemporaries argued, but from all sin (see A.C. III, p. 30, for a review of some of the contemporary positions).

In later discussions the work of Christ is often described in a threefold manner. He had a *prophetic* role to proclaim the divine purpose and urge acceptance. This he did through his incarnation and continues to do through the church. He had a *priestly* role which he fulfilled first of all in his self sacrifice. Here the themes of his active and passive obedience appear. In his active obedience he fulfilled the law—showing the true goal of the ceremonial law, reaffirming the judicial law, and restoring the moral law. In his passive obedience he suffered and died for us. His priestly role includes also the task of making intercession, for believers and for all.

Finally he had a *kingly* role. While this was not exercised openly during the incarnation, but hidden or laid aside, the ascended Christ now rules over the world in the kingdom of power, over the church in the kingdom of grace, and over heaven in the kingdom of glory.[2] He shall come with glory at the last times to judge and restore (A.C. XVII, p. 38) .

Come, Holy Spirit

What do the Confessors have to say about God the Holy Spirit? There is no separate article on the Holy Spirit in the Augsburg Confession, nor in the other statements, unless one wishes to consider the explanations in the catechisms as special articles. Why this omission? First, it is possible that the Lutherans simply had no interest in the Spirit! This is a common attack among some persons who are interested in neo-pentecostalism today. They see their concern and actions as needed correctives to earlier neglect. Another possible reason for the lack of a separate article has to do with the nature of confessional writing. The documents are occasional pieces, i.e., they address areas that are in controversy, particularly with sixteenth-century Roman Catholics. There simply was no significant disagreement with this group, and therefore the matter was not addressed.

The second possibility is certainly the correct one, for the pages of the Confessions, in spite of having no particular article, do demonstrate a great interest and concern with the work of the Spirit of God. For example, where the Confessions insist that apart from Christ, the mirror of the Father's heart, we would only have known God as angry judge, they go on to say, "But neither could we know anything of Christ, had it not been revealed by the Holy Spirit" (L.C., p. 419) . Without the work of Christ, God the Father would not be known to us; without the work of the Holy Spirit, Christ would not be known to us; without the work of the Holy Spirit, Christ would not be known, nor could his promise be accepted (S.C. II, p. 345) .

A summary of this work is found in the Large Catechism:

> Neither you nor I could ever know anything of Christ, or believe in him and take him as our Lord, unless these were first offered to us and bestowed on our hearts through the preaching of the Gospel by the Holy Spirit. The work is finished and completed, Christ has acquired and won the treasure for us by his sufferings, death, and resurrection, etc. But if the work remained hidden and no one knew of it, it would have been all in vain, all lost. In order that this treasure might not be buried but put to use and enjoyed, God has caused the Word to be published and proclaimed, in which he has given the Holy Spirit to offer and apply to us this treasure of salvation. Therefore to sanctify is nothing else than to bring us to the Lord Christ to receive this blessing, which we could not obtain by ourselves (L.C., p. 415) .

The Confessors are convinced, on the basis of the New Testament, of certain affirmations about the Holy Spirit. The personal terms and verbs used, notably in the Gospel of John, convinced them that it was correct to consider the Spirit as a *person* along with the other persons of the Trinity, rather than an influence. This person is God (Acts 5:1-5, where to lie to the Holy Spirit is to lie to God), who worked in creation as a part of the Trinity (Genesis 1:2), but whose primary task is sanctification. As the Small Catechism puts it,

> I believe that by my own reason or strength I cannot

believe in Jesus Christ, my Lord, or come to him. But the Holy Spirit has called me through the Gospel, enlightened me with his gifts, and sanctified and preserved me in the true faith, just as he calls, gathers, enlightens, and sanctifies the whole Christian church on earth and preserves it in union with Jesus Christ in the one true faith (S.C. p. 345).

In the history of Protestantism the word "call" sometimes has been the subject of debate. Four words summarize, for Lutherans, the characteristics of the Holy Spirit's gracious invitation. First the call is *universal,* it is intended for all, because God "desires all men to be saved and to come to the knowledge of the truth" (1 Timothy 2:4).

It is necessary to assert this aspect because some persons, believing that God has decided against certain individuals from all eternity, say that when such outcasts hear the call of the gospel, it is not meant for them, but only for the elect, those whom God has chosen.

Second, the call is described by Lutherans as *efficacious* or powerful. God is at work by this invitation, supplying all that is needed for sinners to embrace Christ, to receive the promise. This is important for our understanding of what a person can do apart from Christ. Given the seriousness of sin and inability of mankind "in the presence of God," it is not realistic to speak about how I can turn myself to God, that I can decide for Christ. The promise and call of God are brought by the Spirit and "the unspiritual [natural] man does not receive the gifts of the Spirit of God, for they are folly to him, and he is not able to understand them because they are spiritually discerned" (1 Corinthians 2:14).

While a human being cannot turn to God by personal, innate capability, everything necessary to accept the promise, to respond to the invitation is given in the call itself. God is himself active in this moment of address and invitation (F.C.S.D. XI, p. 621).

The call is, in the third instance, *serious.* Once again the point of disagreement is with those who feel that God has already decided, both for some and against others, and that therefore when those who are already cast off happen to hear the call of God it is not meant seriously for them. The Lutherans assert that when God calls, he means it, he intends that there be a response.

Sometimes one is called, but does not respond. This indicates, finally, that the call is *resistible* (F.C.S.D. XI, p. 623). Some persons would argue that when God decides, his will cannot be resisted; his grace is irresistible. Lutherans have generally argued against this type of compulsion, and for the element of responsibility, not only for responding positively, but also for saying no to God.

The basic theme in these four characteristics is *power.* God gives power; he works powerfully. The Holy Spirit makes unwilling persons willing, persuades and gives power (F.C.S.D. III, p. 538). This serious, and universal and resistible invitation brings power and is itself efficacious (for some summary passages, see F.C.S.D. II, p. 526).

In describing the work of the Spirit, the Confessions often use the word *awakens* or some synonym for it. Through the Spirit's work one is made aware of need, or, of guilt. One is confronted with what it means to be standing "in the presence of God." After the great sermon of Peter in Acts 2:14 the listeners responded, "What must we do?" So one is still confronted by God, and is made aware of the situation.

Another way of speaking of this work is to say that the Holy Spirit deepens knowledge. There is a movement from head to heart, a recognition that goes deeper than the intellectual agreement that a problem exists. There is a movement from impersonal to personal knowledge, a shift from believing that all persons are involved to an awareness that I am. A movement from general to specific knowledge. Not only is the whole world sinful and the object of God's love, but so am I. Finally a shift from death to life (John 5:24, 11:25; Romans 6. All this is included in *awakening*.

The story of Nathan confronting King David illustrates this. David had sinned and taken the wife of a neighbor, arranging that the neighbor, one of his soldiers, be put in a battle location where he would be killed. Nathan the prophet came to the king and told a story about a rich man with great flocks, who had taken the only sheep of his neighbor. What did the king think should be done to the rich man? David replied, "He should be killed," and the prophet answered, "You are the man." This is one of the most moving and powerful stories in Scripture. "You are the man." When the Spirit deepens knowledge and makes me aware, I realize I am the one who needs forgiveness. When I am called and awakened, my knowledge of myself "in the presence of God" is moved from head to heart, from impersonal to personal, from general to particular. And this all can lead from death to life.

Two courses are open to me when awakening has occurred, when I have become aware of my condition. I may continue to rely in some way upon myself and attempt to make restitution, or appeal the divine verdict. This, futile as it is, leads inevitably to despair. Second, I can see the end of my abilities and turn to the promise of God in Christ; I can repent.

Repentance, in the terms used by the Confessors, includes *cognition* (an awareness and admission that God is right and that I am wrong), *contrition* (fear and sorrow in the presence of God), and *faith* "which strengthens, sustains and quickens the contrite" (Apol. XII, p. 186).

It also includes *aversion,* the willingness and intent to break with known sin (F.C.S.D. V, p. 559). Many persons accept quite easily the notions of cognition and contrition, but aversion, turning away from sin, seems to be another matter. The Confessors speak of the struggle that marks the Christian life. One part of this continuing conflict relates to our turning away from those things which continue to claim us and attract us, but which we know are contrary to what we are called to be in Christ.

The Holy Spirit brings one to faith. One not only accepts God's promise as true, but commits oneself to it. This involves both the head and heart, the entire person. Saving faith commits the self to Christ; it yields, on the basis of personal confrontation, and enters personal relationship with another. It is not simply to accept cognitively something as true, but it is to trust, to commit oneself to another person. This is what the Spirit brings about in his calling, gathering, and awakening.

The work of the Spirit also includes *sanctification* and *preservation.* The person who has been graciously brought into the relationship is now preserved in it. The Small Catechism speaks of calling, gathering, enlightening, and sanctifying (S.C. p. 345).

The Large Catechism puts it like this:

Meanwhile, since holiness has begun and is growing daily, we await the time when our flesh will be put to death, will be buried with all its uncleanness, and will come forth gloriously and arise to complete and perfect holiness in a new, eternal life. Now we are only halfway pure and holy. The Holy Spirit must continue to work in us through the Word, daily granting forgiveness. In that life are only perfectly pure and holy people, full of goodness and righteousness, completely freed from sin, death, and all evil, living in new, immortal, and glorified bodies. All this, then is the office and work of the Holy Spirit, to begin and daily to increase holiness on earth through these two means, the Christian church and the forgiveness of sins. Then, when we pass from this life, he will instantly perfect our holiness and will eternally preserve us in it by means of the last two parts of this article (L.C., p. 418).

What is the basis for justification? Once more we turn to Luther:

Here in the Creed we have the entire essence of God, his will, and his work exquisitely depicted in very short but rich words. In them consists all our wisdom which surpasses all the wisdom, understanding, and reason of men. Although the whole world has sought painstakingly to learn what God is and what he thinks and does, yet it has never succeeded in the least. But here you have everything in richest measure. In these three articles God himself has revealed and opened to us the most profound depths of his fatherly heart, his sheer, unutterable love. He created us for this very purpose, to redeem and sanctify us (L.C., p. 419).

The basis for justification and its synonyms, in summary, is first, the "sheer, unutterable love" of the Father; second, Christ's work which accomplishes all for us and shows the Father's heart; and third, the Holy Spirit, who makes Christ's redemptive work present and operative in our lives, who makes relationship possible, persuades us to trust the God who promises, and who keeps us in the fellowship of faith and new life.

5   The Need for Justification

Once again we add to our circular outline:

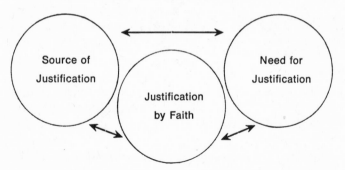

The readings for this chapter are listed in this circle:

What's Wrong with Mankind

Not everyone holds to the notion of justification by faith; not everyone in the world believes in God, Father, Son, and Holy Spirit; but from the time man began leaving records of himself and his religions, we have, in various ways and in different degrees, shown an awareness that something is wrong with us. This is a basic theme in the history of the human race. Reflective persons recognize anxiety and guilt, repentance, and remorse, and have questioned their sources.

Dramatists, those who hold the mirror up to life, speak in different ways of a tragic flaw in man. Aeschylus, Shakespeare, O'Neill, and Williams—all return to this theme. Arthur Miller in *After the Fall* has one of his characters, Quentin, visiting a concentration camp, exclaim, "Who can be innocent again on this mountain of skulls? I'll tell you what I know. My brothers died here, but my brothers built this place! Our hearts cut these stones."

Probers of the human spirit—like Freud, Jung, Adler, Erik Erikson, and Norman Brown—have looked at us. What do the psychiatrists find? What do they deal with? Why are they in business? They deal with fear and hostility and guilt.

Look to another reflective group—theologians. What concerned persons like St. Paul and Augustine, Thomas and Luther, Kierkegaard and Niebuhr? They differ on human nature, the cause and the remedy, but almost without exception there is agreement on the existence of a flaw, an ailment, a destructive force.

Humans are at odds with themselves and thus abusive of themselves and of the world and of their fellows. This is the general topic of our study in this section, seen from the perspective of the Lutheran Confessions.

Although there are many shades and degrees within

each position, there are only a limited number of contemporary views of mankind. One of them is optimistic. The optimist believes that mankind is basically good, and that, given enough time and enough good will, things will work out. We have problems and troubles, but they are based frequently on misunderstandings or a lack of knowledge. If we apply ourselves and strive to be humane persons and use our rational capacities, things are going to get better.

There is a theme of goodness in the cultural history of mankind that supports this view. It was most pointedly expressed in the Victorian era, when things seemed to be going very well indeed. An old cliché says it well. "Every day in every way I'm getting better and better." The optimistic view has some support, but it does not deal adequately with the massive evidences of mankind's cruelty, its viciousness. There is no real room in this system for the Inquisition, or for Buchenwald, or the profit motive as it works its way out in pollution and war.

Some have reacted to this view and to the world and have become pessimistic. Many consistent pessimists hold that man is basically evil, an animal that has emerged from the swamp and jungle to acquire a thin veneer of civilization which always peels away in time of stress and crisis. Since life is characterized by a stream of crisis situations, the future is only chaos. This position takes the existence of evil in the world and in us with utmost seriousness. But just as the consistent optimist is hard pressed to explain evil in the world, so the consistent pessimist has no way to explain the genuinely altruistic and humanitarian activities of persons, not just Christians, but others as well. People sometimes do good, even marvelous, things to and for each other.

Against these two positions I would like to suggest

what I understand to be a biblical view of mankind. Scripture attempts to take both good and evil seriously. The writers speak about goodness in life—not goodness in some sweet by and by, but that life itself is good. Life, the created order, is the work of God; although man is fallen, God still deals graciously with him. At the same time, Scripture speaks clearly about evil. However you wish to interpret the narratives of the Fall, the Scriptures say that man is less than he was intended to be, less than he is intended to be today. Evil is always present; not even Christians are exempt from its activity and presence.

The biblical word most commonly used to describe evil in and among us is *sin*. While moral, legal, psychiatric, and sociological meanings are helpful they do not have the same emphasis as the biblical concept, which is basically religious and personal. As a religious word *sin* is descriptive of a lack of, or breaking of, a relationship with a personal God. As a personal word it describes a lack of trust in another. Luther saw it as the state of being "curved in upon oneself"; Augustine as being "curved to the earth."

The essence of sin for the Lutheran Confessors is broken fellowship. It represents a genuine defection from God. It involves unbelief, and is characterized by egocentricity that expresses itself in pride—pride of power, of knowledge, of virtue, even spiritual pride. This last is of special significance for religious people. Mankind is dependent by nature; sin in this context is a lust for an inappropriate independence.

The Bible defines sin in both moral and religious terms. The religious dimension of sin is man's rebellion against God, his effort to usurp the place of God. The moral and social dimension of sin is injustice. The ego which falsely makes itself the center of existence in its pride and will-to-power inevitably subordinates other life to its will and thus does injustice to other life.[1]

Sin for both the biblical and confessional writers expresses more than the individual in relationship to God. It is also a corporate term. There is massive reference to the solidarity of mankind in sin. We are not free agents, but are somehow involved in a racial catastrophe. Many Old Testament scholars believe that the word "Adam" is not a reference to an individual, but rather to "mankind." The corporate nature of sin presents problems for many so-called modern persons, for we tend to think individualistically, while the biblical understanding is collective.

The collective understanding, as opposed to the individualistic, has received unintentional support from modern depth psychology, which argues that beneath that part of our personality which could be termed "conscious" there is the "subconscious," and deeper still, the "collective unconscious." The levels of subconscious and collective unconscious are not speculative constructs, according to this position, but are based on clinical observation and analysis of dreams, patterns of thought, and symbols which are common to all types of persons in varying civilizations. There is, in the deeper areas, a shared community with other persons even though in the "conscious" mind individualism may be the dominant view.

The way in which the Lutheran Confessions speak of the solidarity of mankind in evil is by the term *original sin*. This term is not an attempt to explain the situation, but to describe it. The basic assertion is that acts of sin, the evil deeds that I do, spring from a solidarity of sin, a condition which is a part of the inheritance of the human race. In this context, sin is inevitable; it is not chosen or rejected. One has no option but to participate in it. On the other hand, sin is not necessary, for then man would be simply an object with no responsibility. But man is responsible.

The genuinely paradoxical character of the Christian understanding of sin is that it insists on some sort of qualified human freedom, and therefore for responsibility despite inevitability. The arguments to support this position are based on experience rather than logical categories. Seen from the outside and described in logical categories, the position leads to simple determinism, where everything is programmed in advance and we are without responsibility. From an interior view, however, experience looks to the rationalizations, the processes of self-deception that go with sin. This does not allow for a simple determinism. The act of sin often involves conscious rebellion and dishonesty. This means that there is some element of responsibility. "The fact of responsibility is attested to by the feelings of remorse or repentance which follows a sinful action." [2] Both remorse and repentance imply responsibility. The first is expressive of freedom without faith and is the basis for future sin; the second expresses freedom and faith, and is the "godly sorrow" of which the Confessions speak.

A Positive View of Mankind

What do the Confessions have to say about mankind? We should start with the positive side, if for no other reason than the fact that certain types of theology seem to say that *nothing* good can be said about human beings. It is possible to so emphasize the fact of sin as to be almost mute regarding the good in man, to be so concerned with bringing persons to recognize their need of a savior, as to imply that we are collectively nothing but a "mass of corruption," as Augustine put it. In this way of thinking the words "total corruption," so prominent in some Protestant thought, are extended to cover everything about us, rather than describing us "in the presence of God," apart from Christ.

It is possible and proper to speak affirmatively about mankind, even apart from Christ. Even after the Fall man is the creation of God. "These passages indicate clearly that even after the Fall God is man's creator who creates body and soul for him" (F.C.S.D. I, p. 514). God has created me, not just the race, the universe, the world, but me (L.C., p. 412). He sustains me. Though there has been a genuine defection, man always remains a being for whom God cares, protects, and whom he blesses.[3]

I read some graffiti, ascribed to a ten-year-old child:

I am me

I am good

'cause God don't make no junk.

We are persons of value, even apart from relationship with God in Christ.

Another positive dimension noted by the Confessions is that man continues to be in the "image of God," when this phrase is used broadly. In the midst of a harsh description of sin and its effects there is the affirmation, ". . . not that man since the Fall is no longer a rational creature, or that he is converted to God without hearing and meditating upon the divine Word, or that in outward or external secular things he cannot have a conception of good or evil or freely choose to act or not to act" (F.C.S.D. II, p. 524). We are rational, creative, and in a certain sense, free persons. We have retained the "image of God," in the broad sense, and are persons of value.

It is man, fallen man, who is described in the Scriptures as being "only a little lower than the angels and crowned with glory and honor" (Psalm 8:5). Mankind, though apart from God, suffering from a genuine defection and alienation, still has dominion over the rest of the created order.

For all these reasons it is proper to speak of the value of man; it is proper to rejoice in the genuine achievements of the human race, to wonder at the accomplishments of humankind, in medicine, art, music, philanthropy. If you have any imagination at all, you cannot help but stand in awe, not simply before what God has done in Jesus Christ, but also before what is done in the world, in the created order. Awe and thankfulness are marks of a Christian person—at all times. There is genuine goodness in the world, and we need not stop to ask if it is always being done by a Christian before we are grateful for it and praise it.

It is proper to speak of value. The other side of this is that it is improper to speak of "total corruption," of sin, if it means that the essence, the essential character of man is sin. Some Lutherans, with the positive intention of magnifying the significance of the work of Christ, went so far as to identify the inner stuff, the essential character of mankind with sin. This suggestion was rejected by the Confessions (F.C. I). Sin is not a part of our essential nature, nor is it a part of God's intention for us in creation. It is a reality, with desperate consequences in us and the whole world, but it is not what we are made for, it is added on, it is an intrusion, and not part of our essential character.

Is it possible for a Lutheran to speak positively of mankind even apart from Christ? We have seen it done.

Mankind is the creation of a loving God, and even after the Fall is the object of love and sustenance. He is still in the image of God, creative, with some freedom. He is still the crown of creation and has dominion over the creation.

The Negative View: Sin

But now the negative word: mankind is the creation of God—but yet is corrupted, something less than intended. The New Testament has several words which are translated *sin:* lawlessness, transgression, trespass, disobedience, ignorance, missing the mark, unrighteousness, godlessness. These words all convey the idea that what is involved is the will of one set against another; most speak in terms of some sort of act (except possibly "missing the mark" and "ignorance"). They are personal and negative acts. Sin is basically conceived of in terms of relationship, or lack of it.

These personal, negative acts have effects, both on the individual and on the relationship between God and man. Sin tends to blind the sinner. Sin involves a gradual loss of moral perception and discernment. One becomes like the fish that live always in the deep recesses and constant blackness of caves and whose eyes eventually cease to function. If light is not used, it is lost, and one becomes used to darkness. One becomes less and less sensitive to the good, the beautiful, until the "senseless mind is darkened" (Romans 1:21). If sin tends to blind, it also enslaves, it binds (Romans 6:16).

Enslavement also is described as being progressive. One is more and more tightly bound until finally there is no escape. Have a friend tie your hands together with one loop of inexpensive string. See if you can break free. Nothing to it! Now try it with three loops—still easy. Now once more, only this time with twenty loops. Break

it! Impossible. In a sense sin's progressive nature in binding is like this.

The final effect of sin on the individual is destruction.
Sin destroys. God is not mocked; it is possible to reap
destruction (Galatians 6:7-8).

How does sin effect the God-man relationship? On
man's part the defection results in fear (Genesis 3:8).
Insofar as one is aware that there is a God, before whom
one is responsible, the result of defection is fear. The
reaction of God to sin is offense and displeasure. "Behold,
the Lord's hand is not shortened, that it cannot save, or
his ear dull, that it cannot hear; but your iniquities have
made a separation between you and your God, and your
sins have hid his face from you so that he does not
hear" (Isaiah 59:1-2). The psalmist recognizes the crisis
and petitions, "Cast me not away from thy presence, and
take not thy Holy Spirit from me" (Psalm 51:11). While
God is consistently pictured as loving the sinner, the
Bible teaches that he hates and punishes sin. It brings
offense and displeasure.

Where does it lead? The key word in the biblical
analysis is *death*. Sin leads to death. If life is conceived
of essentially in terms of relationship, death means separation. This concept seems to be on three levels for the
scriptural writers, each of them tied to sin. They speak
first of all of *spiritual* death, which means to be separated, alienated from God in this life. This is emphasized where the Bible speaks of once being dead in sin,
but now alive in Christ (Ephesians 2:1, 5). There is also
physical death, which the biblical writers describe as the
separation of soul and body. Finally, the Scriptures and
the Confessions speak at times of *eternal* death, everlasting separation from God. Descriptions of judgment
with eternal consequences are found in many places in
the Scriptures (e.g., Matthew 25:46; cf. A.C. XVII, p. 38).

While one might wish that it were not so, God will not force those who choose not to be in relationship with him now, to enter it in the future. In this sense, even separation is to be seen as a means by which he honors his creature, not denying the freedom to say no, even to the end.

What could possibly move one to such serious and self-destructive action? Both the Scriptures and the Confessions note three powerful stimuli to sinful acts, a triumvirate of forces that lead me to evil: the world, the devil, and the flesh.

When they speak of world, they are not referring to mankind or the created order as such, but to that order of things which is opposed to God. The world is a stimulus to sin because of its example and by its active invitation that I conform with it and its ways. The pressure not to be different from the majority, to bow to the suggestion that if you want to be *somebody* in society you have to live a particular way, are examples of solicitation by the world that lead to sin.

A second stimulus to sin is the devil. The Confessions follow the scriptural witness, where the existence of a personal force of evil is assumed and pictured as tempter (Matthew 4:3), deceiver (Ephesians 6:11), ensnarer (2 Timothy 2:26), and liar (Acts 5:3). The most generally used term is adversary.

Is it possible to live in the twentieth century and still believe that such a personal force of evil, such an adversary exists? I believe that it is. The superstitions of other eras, when thunderstorms, rustlings in the attic, colic in cows, and miscarriages all were seen as manifestations of the demonic, need not control us. Some things happen in life, even things that are out of the ordinary, that need not be ascribed either to the divine or the demonic. I am not a first- or sixteenth-century person, but I still recognize the existence and activity of a personal force of evil; I recognized it in the witness of the Scriptures, in the tradition of the Christian community, and in experience itself. The Confessors assert that we are moved to sin by the power of the adversary.

Finally, they argue that we are moved to sin by the flesh, by lusts which are manifestations of the flesh. The Epistle of James puts it,

> Let no one say when he is tempted, "I am tempted by God"; for God cannot be tempted with evil and he himself tempts no one; but each person is tempted when he is lured and enticed by his own desire. Then desire when it has conceived gives birth to sin; and sin when it is full-grown brings forth death (James 1:13-15).

The Confessions do not teach the old Greek idea that the spirit of a person was good, and the body bad. They hold to what has been called an "anthropology of the whole man," that the whole person has fallen into sin and in Christ is redeemed. In the Christian sense, *spirit* is a reference to the whole person insofar as one is in Christ, and *flesh* is a reference to the whole person apart from Christ. We are tempted by the flesh, by that part of us which is not attuned to God and his purposes for us. Flesh and its manifestations are not passive, but active.

One further point: where one might speak of the world and the devil as being exterior forces and stimuli, the flesh refers to something within us, internal drives contrary to the will of the loving Father. This third stimulus expresses a condition within each of us. This leads us to what the articles on sin in the Confessions wish to emphasize—sin as condition. Their term for this is *original sin*.

Sin as a Condition

Article II of the Augsburg Confession can be outlined briefly in this way:

Original Sin—Sin as Condition

      I. Origin: "since the fall of Adam"

     II. Universality: "all men"

   III. Nature: "born in sin"
        A. "Without fear and trust in God"
        B. "With concupiscence"

   IV. Consequence: "condemnation"

    V. Remedy: "born again by baptism and the Holy Spirit"

The primary intent of the writers is to describe the situation in which they found themselves rather than trying to explain in any detail how the situation came into being. The concern is to describe and emphasize the gulf that exists between God and man, to point up the reality of the defection and its alienation and enmity.

This was not a popular topic among their contemporaries, nor is it today. We always attempt to minimize the difference, to bridge the gulf, to explain it away by making it seem less serious than it really is. An optimistic view of mankind is not satisfied with the darkness of the picture. It tries to lighten the shadows by many devices. Some call sin by other names, although this makes as much sense as insisting that lung cancer is a slight case of bronchitis. Some concentrate only on themes such as the Fatherhood of God, the brotherhood of man, and immortality of the soul.

In avoiding this, we are indebted to a movement called Neo-Orthodoxy, which reacted to the liberal optimism of certain nineteenth-century theologians. Aided by a rediscovery of Kierkegaard, Luther, and Calvin, it rediscovered the seriousness of sin, both personal and corporate.

One final question before we turn to the outline: Why do the Confessors spend so much time on this subject? Melanchthon answers quite simply:

> Recognition of original sin is a necessity, nor can we know the magnitude of the grace of Christ unless we acknowledge our faults. All the righteousness of man is mere hypocrisy before God unless we acknowledge that of itself the heart is lacking in love, fear, and trust in God (Apol. II, p. 104) .

The key words in this include *of itself*. What can the heart do of itself? Is there a free will that can turn us to God of itself?

Those who limit or weaken the concept of sin provide the context for the discussion. The main targets for the confessional writers included the Swiss reformer, Zwingli, who held that original sin was only a weakness and did not involve guilt. Some of the Anabaptists denied its existence altogether, holding that children were holy and innocent and that sin was only a violation of a known commandment. Finally their Catholic contemporaries were seen to be in error in their lessened emphasis on guilt and the assertion that original sin was mainly a loss, a privation of original righteousness, with man still capable of some action toward God.

Two things are apparent in the Confessors' description of the origin of sin. One, they are sure that the Fall was a historical event, participated in by individuals, and two, they do not wish to go into any sort of detail in analyzing that fact. Their restraint in the matter is very helpful, and mirrors the biblical approach. Modern, detailed pictures of the Fall often draw much more from John Milton's epic poem *Paradise Lost,* than from the Scriptures. If we wish for more than a subdued and rather shadowy picture, one must go to either intertestamental or to late medieval literature.

The Confessors do manage to say quite a bit about what it was like before a fall into sin and alienation. Since no one was on the scene taking notes, it is appropriate to question the source of their description of what is termed original righteousness. How do they know what it was? By a process of logical deduction. We analyze the situation in which we find ourselves now and contrast this with what it must have been when, after creation, God is described as looking at what had been done, and, "Behold, it was very good" (Genesis 1:31).

What is the situation? What are the characteristics of "natural man," man apart from Jesus Christ, today? He does not fear God or know him; he doesn't trust in God and is unable to yield these affections. He is certainly not a person who has options when it comes to deciding for or against God, so he does not, in this sense, have free will. This is how things are in a condition of sin. How must they have looked when God saw that it was "very good"?

It must have been, Luther, Melanchthon and their friends conclude, that mankind had knowledge of God, fear of God, confidence in God, the power to yield to these affections, and free will (Apol. II, pp. 102-103). Properly speaking, this is what comprises the image of God. We have already noted that image of God in a broad sense refers to rationality and creativity; in a more precise usage, it is equal to original righteousness and consists in the items noted above.

If these comprised mankind's original characteristics, it was easy to see why God would have thought them to be "very good." It is also easy to see why it could be asserted that mankind could have fellowship with God. What is needed for this fellowship? At the very least you have to know who God is; you cannot relate to someone you've never known. You have to be able to trust him, to have confidence in him. And you have to have some degree of freedom that is necessary when dealing with a personal being. There must be a possibility of genuine choice.

What then is the cause of the Fall? The Confessors say that this is a mystery. They do not analyze the original temptation in any detail other than to assert that it hinges on a misuse of free will. They are absolutely sure of one other thing, however, and that is that God cannot be faulted for the disaffection. To assert that God is the cause of sin would posit contradictory qualities, attributes, attitudes, and intentions within God. When the Scriptures assert that God abhors sin, it is not possible that he created it, or that he created man in order that he might sin. They conclude that the cause of sin is the will of the wicked, the devil, the ungodly men, not God (Apol., XIX).

When faced by the question about who is affected by the disastrous consequences of sin, who is involved in sin as condition, the Confessions answer quite directly—everyone, except Jesus Christ.[4] Everyone else is involved in sin.

This is not too difficult to believe when you look critically at the adults around you; it becomes more difficult for some people when infants and young children are concerned. Aren't infants good by nature, or at best neutral? Don't we come trailing clouds of glory, as it were, or with a mind like a blank tablet waiting for information? If this were true, sinning would be something one learned. If we are born good, or without inclination, then doing evil must be learned. And one can also learn not to do and be evil.

But is it necessary to teach children to sin? Is it necessary to teach an only child who has been loved and protected and cherished to be hateful and even destructive of a new baby who comes into the home? It is not necessary. A psychologist might approach the question differently and assert that the response of the child in this situation was natural. Everyone has certain territorial needs, certain requirements for affection; the child had been displaced and was striking back. From a theological perspective it remains an interesting question: If the child is good or neutral, where did he learn to hate and hurt? No one has taught him that in his protected home, and yet he does it—naturally. *It is natural,* but the question is whether nature is neutral, or correct, or whether it too is a manifestation of what we would call sin.

The Confessors assert the universality of the condition of sin. An important passage in their consideration is found in Romans 5 where Paul writes, "Therefore as sin came into the world through one man and death through sin, and so death spread to all men because all men sinned . . ." (Romans 5:12). This passage asserts the universality of sin; it does not explain how it got to all persons.

This lack of precision has brought forth a variety of interpretations. Some persons have stressed that it must mean that our first parents set a bad example, which we all follow. Death, in this context, is the result of each person's freely chosen acts. This position strongly emphasizes our responsibility, and our capability to avoid sin. It is sometimes identified with Pelagius. Another interpretation speaks in terms of inherited guilt. Adam was the head of the race, and all therefore sinned when he did. Therefore all are guilty in him, and suffer the penalty of death. Still another view is that the passage speaks of inherited corruption, or of a condition which is ours. Adam, as the first person, has determined our heredity. The Fall, in this context, means a corruption of human nature which is transmitted to the race. A final interpretation holds that the story is an allegory. Adam is a type of every person. Each of us falls as a matter of personal experience.

The Confessors clearly favor a "conditional" interpretation of the passage and understanding of how sin is transmitted. The point of the passage seems to be to describe sin as both act and condition (Romans 6:6, 12, 14, 17, 22; 7:8, 9, 11, 13, 20, 23).

The nature of the sin of condition is described in both positive and negative ways. First, it means a lack of something, a negation of something. What has been lost, as noted earlier, is original righteousness, which

> was intended to involve not only a balanced physical constitution, but these gifts as well: a surer knowledge of God, fear of God, trust in God, or at least the inclination and power to do these things. This the Scripture shows when it says that man was created in the image of God and after his likeness (Gen. 1:27). What else is this than that a wisdom and righteousness was implanted in man that would grasp God and reflect him, that is, that man received gifts like the knowledge of God, fear of God, and trust in God? (Apol. II, pp. 102-103).

> To make ourselves clear, we are naming these gifts knowledge of God, fear of God, and trust in God. From this it is evident that the ancient definition says just what we do when we deny to natural man not only fear and trust of God, but also the gifts and power to produce them (*Ibid.*, p. 103).

It is quite clear to the Confessors that free will, conceived in a certain way, has been another casualty of sin. One characteristic of life apart from God in Jesus Christ is the inability to turn to God and to move toward the establishment of relationship (Apol. XVIII; F.C. II).

The basic question in this discussion is whether one is describing mankind, in "the presence of other men" or "in the presence of God." To begin with, "in the presence of men" everyone has some liberty to choose to obey the civil law and do the works which reason directs. In matters that are on a par with me, or beneath me I do have free will, the ability to make genuine choices. I can choose, for example, my own candidate for public office; I can decide on whether I will obey traffic laws, whom I will marry, and what I will wear. The Reformers allow for much greater freedom than behaviorist psychologists do today.

The basic problem, however, is, do I have comparable freedom before God? The Confessors state that the natural person, the person apart from Christ, has no power to work spiritual righteousness, to move toward God. This type of righteousness, they insist, is wrought in the heart by God alone. Their conviction of this was absolute. They find support for their view in 1 Corinthians 2:14: "The unspiritual man does not receive the gifts of the Spirit of God, for they are folly to him, and he is not able to understand them because they are spiritually discerned." The words, "when you were dead in sin, God made you alive," (Ephesians 2:1) are additional proof. There is no point in talking about the self-resuscitation of a dead person. Another must do it. So also the sinner of himself cannot turn to God. There is no option, no free will.

The Confessions also reject several groups who hold

contrary views: Manicheans, who believe that everything in life is determined by outside forces; Pelagians of every type, who hold that man moves godward by natural powers, or that at least he makes a start and then proceeds with divine assistance; and Synergists, who argue that God makes the beginning; but then man moves by innate capacities.

If something has been lost through sin, something else has been added to our character. This is called concupiscence. The Confessors do not distinguish between "sin" (missing the mark) and "concupiscence," as Paul does in Romans 7. The apostle suggests that sin is dormant until goaded by the law, that it is like a sleeping dog that someone kicks; it then shows itself in covetousness or lust.

The identification of concupiscence and lust by Augustine and medieval theologians has led to some confusion as to what it means for Luther and the Confessors. In their writings the word does not refer primarily to the sensual or sexual. Here is the way they speak of it: "Concupiscence, which pursues carnal ends contrary to the Word of God, is not only the desires of the body, but also carnal wisdom and righteousness in which it trusts while it despises God" (Apol. II, p. 103). "Concupiscence" in this context is associated with the egocentric drive that places the self on the throne rather than allowing God to be God, rather than with sexual misconduct.

The Consequences of Sin

Finally, what is the consequence of the condition and acts of sin? What is the result of the "horrible deep corruption," the source of acts of sin?

We believe, teach and confess that original sin is not a slight corruption of human nature, but that it is so deep a corruption that nothing sound or uncorrupted has survived in man's body or soul, in his inward or outward powers. . . . This damage is so unspeakable that it may not be recognized by a rational process, but only from God's Word (F.C. II, p. 467). It is truly sin, and brings death (A.C. II, p. 29).

Is the condition of sin ever absent from the believer? The Confessors believe not. Sin continues to exist and to threaten and to struggle. Even the Apostle Paul found that sin always lay close at hand and that life was a continual battle (Romans 7:19-24).

There is, however, a solution to the matter of sin. How we describe this remedy will be determined by how we view evil. For example: if sin comes from incorrect thinking, the solution is truth and reason. If its source is ignorance, the solution is knowledge and education. If it relates to the physical body primarily, the solution is asceticism—anything that puts the body down and concentrates on the spirit. If sin originates in and is characterized by incompleteness, the solution is patient waiting for the next stage of evolution. If it is hereditary, the answer is in eugenic manipulation. If in the environment, then we move to change the neighborhood. If sin's source is a misplaced good (in drunkenness, for example), the answer is discipline. If the source is the corrupting influence of civilization, then the solution is to return to nature in a Romantic movement.

All of these cures are based on a basic optimism; some tend to eliminate personal responsibility; some look only to our innate capacities such as reason.

These are not the answers suggested by the Confessors, who argue that sin is condition and act contrary to the will of God and harmful to man. The only corrective, given the seriousness of the situation, is God's grace and forgiveness, as they put it, in baptism and the Holy Spirit. They believe that in baptism, through God's power, the guilt of original sin is removed although the condition remains. The Christian life, though one of constant forgiveness, is a battle. In this struggle the guilt and concupiscence are not reckoned, and the promise is that there will always be strength enough for the battle.

Many pages and words have been devoted to this subject. Why all the concern? Simply put, because diagnosis is the first step to a possible cure; without knowledge of sin there can be no recognition of the need of a Savior. Everything, once again, comes back to a concern for the glory of Christ and our need. The problem with an inadequate view, one that does not take sin seriously, is that it always leads back into a position that does not take Christ seriously and tends to overestimate our contribution. But proper diagnosis is necessary if we're going to be healed. We need to see sin, not as the end, as the last word, but as a necessary intermediate word that opens our ears to the good news of Christ, who is the way from slavery into freedom, from alienation into fellowship, and from death into life.

6   The Means of Justification

Once again our diagram has added a section:

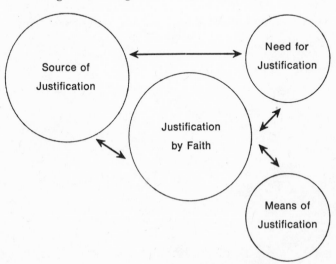

The contents of our newest circle, in abbreviated form, look like this:

Means of Justification
A.C. & Apol. V, VII-XV
S.A. III, ii-xii
P.P.
S.C., L.C.,
    pp. 416-419
        342-344, 365-411
        348-349, 436-446
        351-352, 447-457
        349-351, 457-461
F.C. V-VII, X

The heart of the Lutheran Confessions is relationship, how fellowship with God is established. The basis for this is summarized in the words describing God's "sheer, unutterable love" (L.C. p. 419) as seen in the work of Christ and made known through the Holy Spirit. The need for God's act in Christ lies in the lost and desperate situation of mankind. Now, how does God work, what means are used in reestablishing that which was lost?

Just as in the incarnation, God has chosen to do his saving work through the ordinary things of life, through words, and through people. Rather than speculate on what other routes might have been open to him, the Lutheran Confessors concentrate on what is being done, and by what means. They are convinced that the God who is at once Creator, Savior, and Sanctifier works in the world today by ordinary means.

Interest in the church, the community of the faithful, as a means by which God is active, has increased in recent years. Several factors have contributed to this renewed concern. Recovery of a biblical doctrine of the church, with its understanding that Christians are part of a people, a community of God, rather than simply individuals, has aided.

So has the view that this new community is the best link between persons today and the historical Christ. The church in this context is both proclaimer and guardian of the historical message.

New insight into the social aspect of Christianity is also important. This does not mean that some sort of secularized kingdom of God will come into being, nor that we are to look for some sort of emerging Christian society. Rather it recognizes that the church has responsibilities to society, to evangelize and transform it. The church is seen as a community with a mission to witness and to serve. This has led to a decline of an earlier "triumphalist" view in which the church claimed power to rule the affairs of society.

The discovery that the major Reformers, Luther and Calvin, had high doctrines of the church, and were not advocates of individualism as sometimes claimed, has been of assistance in rekindling interest.

Finally we note how the ecumenical movement has drawn us to closer analysis and appreciation of what the Christian community actually is. There appears to be greater interest today than at any time since the Reformation itself in the meaning and future of the church.

The Historical Context for the Lutheran View

A summary of the confessional view of church and ministry is in the *Augsburg Confession,* Articles V, VII-XV, XXV, and XXVIII. The historical context of the articles is important. Two major positions important in the sixteenth century and today, are opposed. On the one hand, the Enthusiasts, including Thomas Münzer and others of the Anabaptist movement such as Hans

Denk, spoke of a direct line to God by means of which they were instructed to take certain actions, or to avoid others. There was, in this sense, a new revelation from God, often quite apart from the Scriptures, and sometimes even contrary to it.

A basic problem in this approach has to do with some way of evaluating the new message. How do you test the command? Münzer, for example, was quite convinced that God had commanded him to rouse the peasants to overthrow the established order. He warned the rulers, in a sermon on Daniel, that unless they changed their ways they would be killed. God had commanded this of him.

Is this a type of problem related only to earlier centuries? One can visit any mental hospital in the country and find some persons who have actually committed murder or other criminal action, convinced that they had been directed to do so by God. Once again the question remains, how do you test what the voice, or insight has told you? Are our emotions, our internal directives always reliable? Should there not be some means by which our insights are examined, some message which, in the experience of the community, is more reliable than our inner voice? Even if one has dreams, auditions, and visions, what is their source?

Perhaps the Confessors overreact, but their conviction was that God deals with us, as far as we are able to ascertain, through external means. "In these matters," Luther insists,

> which concern the external, spoken Word, we must hold firmly to the conviction that God gives no one his Spirit of grace except through or with the external Word which comes before. Thus we shall be protected from the enthusiasts—that is, from the spiritualists who

boast that they possess the Spirit without and before the Word and who therefore judge, interpret, and twist the Scriptures or spoken Word according to their pleasure. . . . The papacy, too, is nothing but enthusiasm, for the pope boasts that "all laws are in the shrine of his heart," *(Corpus juris canonici,* Book VI, I, c. 1.) and he claims that whatever he decides and commands in his churches is spirit and law, even when it is above and contrary to the Scriptures or spoken Word. . . . Even so the enthusiasts of our day condemn the external Word, yet they do not remain silent but fill the world with their chattering and scribbling, as if the Spirit could not come through the Scriptures or the spoken word of the apostles but must come through their own writings and words (S.A. III, VIII, p. 312).

The only way to be safe is to cling to that Word which God has given through the apostolic witness. "Accordingly, we should and must constantly maintain that God will not deal with us except through his external Word and sacrament" *(Ibid.,* p. 313).

Enthusiasm or the inner light manifests itself today also, not only in psychological aberration posing as revelation, but also in the feeling of persons who say, "I don't care what you believe, as long as you're sincere." Sincerity, in this instance, is taken as a substitute for the gospel. St. Paul is speaking to this situation when he says pointedly, "If anyone is preaching to you a gospel contrary to that which you received, let him be accursed" (Galatians 1:9). A modern writer has put it well, "The proclamation of the church is not what somebody happens to feel strongly about—be it ever so interesting. It is defined by the Gospel, the good news of what God has done in Jesus, the Christ." [1] The Confessors are opposed to "enthusiasm," old or new.

The other major opponent that the articles on ministry face may be termed clericalism. While it seemed in the sixteenth century that Roman Catholicism was most prone to this position, no part of the Christian community has escaped its problems. Here the major issue is once again the basis of fellowship. Is relationship with God based on a personal relationship, or is it based on the work of professional religious persons on your behalf, with a minimum of personal involvement for you? The tension is between personal and professional relationship. Is the priest or pastor the one to work, pray, believe, worship, meditate, serve, on our behalf? Is it enough for the members of a congregation to "pay our dues," and "let the professional do that sort of thing"?

Against this idea, Article V of the Augsburg Confession insists that public ministry is an office which exists so that *people* can come to faith and thus be personally tied to a person, Jesus Christ. We cannot personally relate to another by proxy.

The Keys of the Kingdom

All talk about the church and its ministry is related in some way to the ancient concept of the keys. This was a hotly debated issue in the sixteenth century. The discussion hinges on certain very significant Scripture passages. In Matthew's Gospel we read, "I will give you the keys of the kingdom of heaven, and whatever you bind on earth shall be bound in heaven, and whatever you loose on earth shall be loosed in heaven" (Matthew 16:19; see also 18:18). This is coupled with the authority which our Lord claims for himself:

All authority in heaven and on earth has been given to me. Go therefore and make disciples of all nations,

baptizing them in the name of the Father and of the
Son and of the Holy Spirit, teaching them to observe
all that I have commanded you; and lo, I am with you
always, to the close of the age (Matthew 28:18-19).

Lutherans have always held that the power of the keys is
the power to loose or retain sins, that is, to administer
the treasure of the church, the gospel.[2] Every announcement of the good news of forgiveness, every absolution
depends on this power given by the Lord of the church.

The crucial question, however, remains—to whom was
this power, this authority given? The Roman Catholic
position in the sixteenth century maintained that this
power had been given specifically to the Apostle Peter,
and to those who succeeded him. The keys, in this instance, were the basis for the governing, law-giving power
of the church. Luther asserted first, that this type of
power was never given in the church, and second, that
this mistaken notion was the basis for ecclesiastical and
societal tyranny. At issue are Jesus' words to Peter in
Matthew 16:19: "I will give you the keys of the kingdom of heaven," and whether the confession of faith
made by Peter was his own or a corporate statement of
the apostles. Did Jesus mean that St. Peter would be the
rock upon which the church would stand, or was it the
apostolic faith that would serve as foundation along with
the person of Christ?

This latter interpretation dominated the early Christian community. The church was thought to be built "on
the foundation of the apostles and prophets, Christ Jesus
himself being the cornerstone" (Ephesians 2:20). Already
by the fourth century, however, this foundation role and
authority were being ascribed to the person of Peter and
his successors. This was one of the roots of papal power
in the Middle Ages and succeeding centuries.

In contrast to this, the Confessors insist that the keys, the power and authority to preach the gospel, were given to the church, the community of the faithful. After quoting a series of Bible passages, Melanchthon states,

These words show that the keys were given equally to all the apostles and that all the apostles were sent out as equals. In addition, it is necessary to acknowledge that the keys do not belong to the person of one particular individual but to the whole church, as is shown by many clear and powerful arguments, for after speaking of the keys in Matthew 18:19, Christ said, "If two or three of you agree on earth," etc. Therefore he bestows the keys especially and immediately on the church, and for the same reason the church especially possesses the right of vocation (P.P., p. 324).

In summary, the keys refer to the power to bring the gospel; they are given to the whole church. They include the power and command to preach, forgive and retain sin, and administer the sacraments (A.C. XXVIII, p. 81). The keys have no reference to any sort of legal or law-giving function; the church does not have this role.

Christ gave the apostles only spiritual power, that is, the command to preach the gospel, proclaim the forgiveness of sins, administer the sacraments, and excommunicate the godless without physical violence. He did not give them the power of the sword or the right to establish, take possession of, or transfer the kingdoms of the world (P.P., p. 325).

What Is the Church?

If the responsibilities associated with the keys are given to the church, one must have some conception about what *church* means. The Augsburg Confession describes it as, "the assembly of all believers among whom the Gospel is preached in its purity and the holy sacraments are administered according to the Gospel" (A.C. VII, p. 32). Luther puts it, characteristically, with more color: "Thank God, a seven-year-old child knows what the church is, namely, holy believers and sheep who hear the voice of their Shepherd" (S.A. III, xii, p. 315).

The church, in other words, is people, gathered around and by their Leader, or Shepherd. The church, in this sense, is itself an object of faith. It is constituted by faith, and since this is not subject to rational, empirical analysis, the church belongs to another realm of inquiry and affirmation. When the word church is used precisely, or properly, it refers to an assembly that is not visible, but rather an object of faith. It has certain marks, and where these are present, there the church also exists. Where there is preaching of the gospel, the church is present, for God will not allow his Word to return to him empty (Isaiah 55:10-11). Where there is the visible proclamation of the Word, the sacraments, there the church is also.

"Church" is also used in a more general, and less precise way. Here it may refer to an institution, or a building, or organization. Used properly, or precisely, however, the church is an assembly of those who are in faith relationship with Jesus Christ. It is to this people that the keys are given and through them that this power is exercised (S.A. VII, p. 311).

The Priesthood of All Believers

At least three issues are related to the use of the keys in the church: the priesthood of all believers, the office of public ministry, and the duties of such ministry of Word and Sacrament.

In contrast to the Roman Catholic position in which one becomes a priest by virtue of ordination, the Lutheran Confessors insisted that all Christians are priests by virtue of baptism. There are therefore not two classes of Christians, the priests and non-priests, with two types of power and authority, but rather one assembly of believers, all priests, with a common ministry of worship, witness, service, and if need be, suffering. God has established a holy nation and a kingdom of priests for himself (Exodus 19:5-6; 1 Peter 2:9), and we become a part of it through baptism. It is not only the monks that have a calling from God, as some believed, but every Christian is called to exercise ministry, to serve in that place in society where he or she is found. Every Christian is called to represent God before the people by proclamation, in word and in life, and to represent the people before God, by sacrifice and prayer. The reality and characteristics of this life before God will be discussed in a later chapter.

The Public Ministry

If all Christians are priests before God, with privileges and responsibilities, why do we have pastors in congregations? Why is there an office of public ministry of Word and Sacrament?

While all the believers have rights and responsibilities, they do not exercise them publicly without being called to do so. The administration of the power of the keys is to be done in an orderly fashion. The word "publicly" is of central importance here. It refers not to the distinction between what happens in the privacy of the home and the openness of the community or between what is done alone and in the company of many. The word here refers to what is done "on behalf of the church."

Since the privileges belong to all, the Confessors argue,

no single individual may take them unto himself, without the call of the other believers (A.C. XIV, p. 36). Both Roman Catholic and Lutheran congregations had been bothered by wandering preachers who did come, without call, and preached, often disturbing the people, and just as often fleecing them of their funds before a hasty departure. This was not in accord with a healthy understanding of public ministry, according to the Confessors.

It is necessary, also to have order in the church (1 Corinthians 14:40). While everyone could claim the right to preach, there would be chaos if everyone insisted on exercising this right on a given Sunday. What would happen if thirty people insisted on presiding at the Lord's Supper? For the sake of order, the congregation calls and sets aside someone to do this publicly, on their behalf.

Public ministry exists to assist the people of God to exercise their own ministry, their missionary function. The Reformers are convinced that this ministry is established by God, for the sake of the church. It is not simply a sociological and practical development. It did not evolve when a group of like-minded people sat down and said, "Well, we've got a group here: we need a little organization; let's have a leader." On the contrary they wish to emphasize that ministry is established by God; it is God's intention for the church. We have been commissioned, they argue, to go into all the world (Matthew 28:19-20) and have been given a ministry of reconciliation (2 Corinthians 5:18). It is God who equips the church, "And his gifts were that some should be apostles, some prophets, some evangelists, some pastors and teachers . . ." (Ephesians 4:11). Faith comes from what is heard, and what is heard comes through those whom God has called to preach (Romans 10:14).

Article V of the Augsburg Confession summarizes its understanding of the relevant Scriptures and says simply, "God instituted the office of the ministry." The connection between this position and what had already been stated about how relationship with God is established in Article IV is important. Relationship comes "through faith"; ministry exists "so that this faith may be proclaimed." In another place the Confessors say:

The church has the command to appoint ministers; to this we must subscribe wholeheartedly, for we know that God approves this ministry and is present in it. It is good to extol the ministry of the Word with every possible kind of praise in opposition to the fanatics who dream that the Holy Spirit does not come through the Word but because of their own preparations (Apol. XIII, p. 212; see also A.C., and Apol. XXVIII).

One enters the public ministry by being called to it (A.C. XIV, p. 36). The office has been established by God for the sake of the gospel, and now the church has the responsibility to fill it. The act by which this is done has traditionally been called "ordination." Ordination is the official and public recognition of the call to ministry. It may also be described as the public setting aside of an individual to serve in this way.

Once again, the position becomes clearer when set in the context provided by certain opponents. The Confessors were not satisfied, as we have seen, with the Enthusiasts, who tended to demean the significance of the ministry of the Word and God's use of external means. They also disagreed with their Roman Catholic contemporaries on the nature of ordination and of priesthood. One becomes a priest in the Roman Catholic system by ordination, and thus becomes a sacramental person who is

able to "offer" or sacrifice the Mass (Lord's Supper).
Ordination is thought to effect some sort of interior
change in the nature of the person involved, and to mark
one forever. In theory, "once a priest, always a priest."
One may be denied priestly functions, but remain a
priest, by virtue of ordination.

This contrasts with the position of the Confessors that
one becomes a priest by baptism and ordination means
the assumption of an office within the whole people of
God. This understanding does not demean the pastoral
role, since God himself has established the office of ministry. The work of the ordained person is not geared
completely to the sacraments, but concentrates on the
Word of God in its twofold dimension: proclamation,
and administration of the visible word, the sacraments.
There is certainly a change involved in ordination, but
it is not basically a change in the nature of the persons
involved, but rather a change in function; one has different duties and responsibilities in this form of public
ministry.[3]

Finally, who has the power to ordain? It belongs to the
church, not only to certain officers, such as bishops.

> Since the distinction between bishop and pastor is not
> by divine right, it is manifest that ordination adminis-
> tered by a pastor in his own church is valid by divine
> right. Consequently, when the regular bishops become
> enemies of the Gospel and are unwilling to administer
> ordination, the churches retain the right to ordain for
> themselves. For wherever the church exists, the right
> to administer the Gospel also exists. Wherefore it is
> necessary for the church to retain the right of calling,
> electing, and ordaining ministers. . . . So in an emer-
> gency even a layman absolves and becomes the minister
> and pastor of another (P.P., p. 331).

Some persons deeply involved in some form of lay ministry, seem to feel that every situation is an emergency, and
that therefore any time is the right time for every Christian to function publicly in the ministry of Word and
Sacrament. The Confessors deny this as an option, for
it contradicts the basic notion of the decency and order
about which they speak in Article XIV of the Augsburg
Confession. Emergency situations are not to be made
normative in the church.

There is then, a universal priesthood of believers
which one enters by baptism. Its work might well be
described as the ministry of the whole people of God.
There is also, within this larger ministry, a special enabling office or function, established by God for the sake
of the gospel, entered by a call and ordination. This is
the public ministry of Word and Sacrament.

The Word: Law and Gospel

The duties of this ministry center on preaching and
the administration of the sacraments, both expressions of
the Word of God. Preaching is absolutely central to the
Confessors, although for Luther himself a complete service of worship always had both the sermon and the Sacrament of the Altar. Proclamation is central. The church
is even described at times as a "mouth house," rather
than a "pen house." Emphasis on oral proclamation can
be overdone to the point where one seems to feel that
the only way to reach another person is through the ear.
Nonetheless the understanding that the duties of public
ministry center on the Word of God in its fullness is
appropriate. "Word of God" for the Reformers meant
three things: Jesus Christ (John 1); the Scriptures; and
oral proclamation. The second and third categories are

or become Word, only insofar as, and because they bear witness to the Christ.[4]

The Confessors often speak of the Word as a means of grace. Grace is always associated by these writers with the person and work of God. Its source is God whose actions in creation, in pity, patience, and love toward the undeserving continues to this day. Grace is especially clear in the cross, the great act of deliverance for those at enmity and in bondage (Romans 3:24; 5:20, Ephesians 1:6-7; Galatians 2:21; 4:4-5; Titus 2:11). It is spontaneous; it springs from the very nature of God, rather than being called forth by its object, mankind. It is sovereign and free; it is not necessary. Grace is unmerited. What is offered is either received as a pure and unearned gift, or not at all. Finally, grace is redemptive. God shows his true nature in his redemptive action for the lost.

If these are descriptive words about grace, what can be said about the office of preaching in the New Testament? Why do the Confessors lay such great store by it, even to the point of calling it a means of grace, a means by which God is redemptively active?

The Book of Acts provides some insight and some answers. For one thing, one notes how important preaching was to the infant church. It was the full-time occupation of the apostles, and helpers were secured to enable them to concentrate on it (Acts 6). It was continued even under serious threat. When persecution forced the preachers to move, they simply continued to tell the story in other places (Acts 13). Persons like Paul and Barnabas were chosen by the church and sent out to distant areas with the prime task of preaching the good news (Acts 13).

What happened when the Word was preached? The Book of Acts gives several descriptions: persons are convicted of sin, persuaded to trust, cleansed, made heirs, receive the Holy Spirit, are saved, and are edified.

Finally, to what are these marvelous results credited? Only to the presence of the Holy Spirit. It was not due to the preachers and their oratory, wisdom, rank, or skill. When it seemed they relied on these personal qualities, the results were always less than satisfactory. Only the power of the Spirit could accomplish what had been done. The Word therefore was seen as a tool, a means, a vehicle of the Holy Spirit. It was a means of God's gracious, redemptive action. For this reason Luther and his colleagues were convinced it was proper to assert that the Word was a means of grace.

In reading, preaching, and living, Lutherans have always been deeply concerned with the basic categories of law and gospel. The concern is to distinguish the two, without separating them. Since what is at stake is the work of Christ on our behalf, it is important to consider the distinction in our day.

No one comprehends this distinction once and for all. It must be received again and again. This is true because of our tendency to return to legalism. The whole history of the church illustrates this. Study again the problems Paul faced in the Galatian churches. Reread what happened in the post-apostolic church, or in certain types of scholasticism or pietism. Examine the rules and regulations we establish for ourselves as means of proving our own goodness, or of asserting some kind of hold on God.

The law and gospel must be distinguished, yet not separated. We must see the difference between demand and promise, requirement and fulfillment, burden and freedom, work and gift, wrath and grace, and between death and life. This is what is at stake in the insistent words of the Lutheran Confessions.

The distinction between law and Gospel is an especially brilliant light which serves the purpose that the
Word of God may be rightly divided and the writings
of the holy prophets and apostles may be explained
and understood correctly. We must therefore observe
this distinction with particular diligence lest we confuse the two doctrines and change the Gospel into law.
This would darken the merit of Christ and rob dis-
turbed consciences of the comfort which they otherwise have in the holy Gospel when it is preached
purely and without admixture, for by it Christians can
support themselves in the greatest temptations against
the terrors of the law (F.C.S.D. V, p. 558).

In an earlier writing Melanchthon sounded the same
crucial note.

All Scripture should be divided into these two chief
doctrines, the law and the promises. In some places it
presents the law. In others it presents the promise of
Christ; this it does either when it promises that the
Messiah will come and promises for forgiveness of sins,
justification, and eternal life for his sake, or when, in
the New Testament, the Christ who came promises
forgiveness of sins, justification and eternal life (Apol.
IV, p. 108).

Confusing law and gospel will propel us back into a
religion of merit, into a theology of barter, in which we
try to trade off our obedience to law for the promises
that relate only to the gospel. This can only confuse the
work and merit of Christ and drive us to despair. This
two-fold theme runs throughout the entirety of the Lutheran Confessions.

Law may be described in terms of its origin and its
uses. Without entering into the debate as to whether the

law is rooted in nature, in reason, or in authority, the Confessions posit its origin as a part of creation itself. The law, as they understand it, is based on God's creative will for mankind. The authority of the state, for example, is not accidental or merely the product of man's ingenuity or power; it is rooted in the will of God.

There is no part of creation where God is not present, and where he does not rule. On the one hand he rules graciously, by the gospel. This is the realm or kingdom comprised of his Son, the church "properly speaking." He also rules in the world. Here he acts through the structures of society—home, government, and education, and by means of law. Here he shows both his grace in sustaining and empowering, and also his wrath against sin, by limiting and frustrating the schemes of the world. The state exists for the sake of peace, and that the gospel may have free course. The state establishes its own validity as it lives in accordance with God's moral law, which is God's means of exercising his control over the affairs of mankind (L.C., p. 368).

The Confessions traditionally distinguish between three uses of the law: the civil, theological, and the so-called third use. The civil use relates to the way persons conduct themselves within the structures of society. Put most simply its function here is to restrain the wicked, "by threats and fear of punishment . . ." (S.A. III, ii, p. 303). Against those who hold an optimistic view of human nature Luther argued:

A man who would venture to govern an entire country or the world with the Gospel would be like a shepherd who should place in one fold wolves, lions, eagles and sheep together and let them freely mingle with one another and say, "Help yourselves, and be good and peaceful among yourselves; the fold is open, there is plenty of food; have no fear of dogs or clubs." The sheep, forsooth, would keep the peace and would allow themselves to be fed and governed in peace, but they would not live long, nor would one beast survive another.[5]

Lest this evaluation appear too somber for our modern age, picture what life would be like in any city or group of people if there were no laws, no courts or police. Life would again be a matter of survival of the fittest, strongest, and most ruthless.

The Christian concern with the civil use of the law recognizes that it deals with the second table of the law, our relation to others. Christians respond to the civil use by obeying law, and living as Christs in relation to it. We are to respond also by working to change laws that are unjust, that oppress people, and deprive them of basic justice. We respond by working to get good persons into government. Political structure is seen as a mask behind which and through which God is at work. Finally the Christian responds to the civil use of the law by working to have good laws that are properly, and carefully enforced. Good order and justice are gifts from God. They come to us by human means and are to be appreciated and improved.

Law, in the second instance, has a "theological use." This is the major concern in the relationship between law and gospel. In the New Testament, specifically in the Pauline writings, the basic use of the law is to reveal to the sinner his true condition so that the message of the gospel might be heard and appropriated. Law accuses and condemns; it drives one to an awareness of self "in the presence of God" (Romans 3:19-20; 5:20; 7:7ff.; Galatians 3:24).

Some scholars of the Old Testament have claimed that

Paul has not presented a complete picture of the word "law," or torah in the Old Testament. They note that there it had a more positive thrust, that it meant teaching. This is certainly true, but Paul's theological concern is well taken and is the one which determined the Confessors' view. Law in this context is meant to reveal our need of a Savior.

When the Confessions speak of the theological use of law, they carefully note that they are speaking of the Ten Commandments. "By 'law' in this discussion we mean the commandments of the Decalogue, wherever they appear in the Scriptures. For the present we are saying nothing about the ceremonial and civil laws of Moses" (Apol. IV, p. 108).

The specific portion of the Decalogue which is of primary concern to them is the first table, those commands that describe our relation to God.[6]

The results of the theological use of the law depend on whether or not the Holy Spirit is active through it. Without the Spirit, the law has no effect at all, or it encourages an attempt to become acceptable before God by an outer obedience, specifically to the second table. The person hears a command, "Do this," and responds by trying to do it to please God and make oneself acceptable. When the Spirit is present, the law leads to disturbance, despair in the self, and to repentance (F.C.S.D. II, p. 531). The simplest description of repentance is the combination of sorrow for sin and faith in God (A.C. XII, p. 34). In expanded form it is presented as including the recognition of sin, sorrow for it, and the intention to desist from it (F.C.S.D. V, p. 559).

Lutherans are not "perfectionists." We recognize that sin remains in the believer and we affirm Luther's understanding that the believer is "at the same time justified and sinner," it follows that the theological use of the law always remains in effect. The law continues to show us our failings, our lostness, and continues to drive us to daily repentance. This repentance is a return to our baptismal covenant; it is living one's baptism.

The necessary presence and use of law prevents Lutherans from becoming antinomian, that is, from arguing that law has no place in the life of the Christian. This was one of the problems that led to the writing of the Formula of Concord (FC. VI).

There is considerable debate within Lutheran circles today regarding the so-called third use of the law. If the first is to restrain evil in the civil realm, and the second, to drive persons to see their need of a savior, the third is to guide the believer, the regenerate person, in life. This use has never been a major emphasis in our tradition, and some have questioned whether it is correct or helpful. The question hinges on whether it is necessary to have the law as a guide within a relationship. Do my wife and I, after many years of mutual love and respect, need any outside party to tell us how to act toward each other? Does a healthy fruit tree need to be told to bear fruit? Faith itself, forms the Christian life and it is living, busy and active and responds to the love of God and the needs of the neighbor without external direction (F.C.S.D. IV, pp. 551-552). Others would maintain that the law of God, as a part of his revelation of his continuing will for us, does have a guiding function for the Christian and not simply one of making sin known or of restraining wickedness (F.C. VI). In this context one does not live *under* the law and is thus condemned or driven to obedience, but rather *in* the law. Here one acts not by coercion but in willing response to God's love in Christ.[7]

A wariness of the dangers of returning to legalism and barter theology, plus a concern for the spontaneous nature of the Christian life, have caused some to be silent on the theme of obedience, which is also scriptural (Exodus 19:5-6; Mark 3:35; Luke 6:46).

The law, the *torah* understood as "teaching" expresses God's continuing will for his people. The possibility of misuse should not deny us the benefits of its proper role. Whatever one's position on the third use, there is no doubt that both the first and second uses remain in operation for the Christian. A Lutheran cannot be antinomian.

The law is only a part of what the Scriptures are to bring to the world. The greater, more significant, word is gospel. The Confessors used the word "gospel" to mean "good news," as did the New Testament. The gospel is, "the free promise of the forgiveness of sins for Christ's sake" (Apol. IV, p. 132).

At one point, apparently irritated at seemingly endless debate, the description is put in the context of a prayer:

> O Christ, how long wilt Thou bear these insults with which our enemies attack thy Gospel! In the Confessions we said that the forgiveness of sins is received freely for Christ's sake, through faith. If this is not the true voice of the Gospel, if it is not the statement of the eternal Father which Thou who art in the bosom of the Father has revealed to the world—then the charge against us is true. But thy death is a witness, thy resurrection is a witness, the Holy Spirit is a witness, thy whole church is a witness: this is truly the teaching of the Gospel that we receive the forgiveness of sins not because of our merits but because of Thee, through faith (Apol. XXVII, p. 271).

When the word "gospel" is used precisely, its content describes God's "proper work," what he intends to do—namely, to save. On occasion the word is also used "broadly" and then it contains the entire message of both repentance and forgiveness. This includes preaching of the law, and thus is a part of what the Confessors call God's "alien work," directed at terrifying and thus preparing one for the good news. The major emphasis of the Lutheran Confessions is on the narrow, or proper, use of the word. Here the gospel is set in contrast to the law and is,

> not a proclamation of contrition and reproof, but is strictly speaking, precisely a comforting and joyful message which does not reprove or terrify but comforts consciences that are frightened by the law, directs them solely to the merit of Christ, and raises them up again by the delightful proclamation of God's grace and favor acquired through the merits of Christ (F.C. Ep. V, p. 478).

If the response to law is obedience, to the gospel it is trust, acceptance and commitment. A promise is to be believed; the one who promises is to be trusted, even in the face of apparently contradictory evidence. "Faith is," as the writer to the Hebrews put it, "the assurance of things hoped for, the conviction of things not seen" (Hebrews 11:1). All of life is lived by faith, and thus becomes the proper worship of God. Luther writes,

> This is the very highest worship of God, that we ascribe to Him truthfulness, righteousness and whatever else ought to be ascribed to one who is trusted. Then the soul consents to all his will, then it hallows His name and suffers itself to be dealt with according to God's good pleasure, because, clinging to God's promises, it does not doubt that He, Who is true, just and wise, will do, dispose, and provide all things well.[8]

The promise of God in the gospel, when taken to one-self through the Holy Spirit, has results which almost defy description. The Confessors and others have struggled to present the wealth of this continuing gift and result. All that is described under the concept of "justification by grace through faith" is put in this context. We receive consolation, forgiveness, reconciliation, acceptance, and become heirs (A.C. IV, p. 30; Apol. IV, p. 177; F.C.S.D. III, p. 473).

A more modern writer describes the result as "the courage to be." Others speak of value that is given and recognized. Still others affirm authentic existence as the result of this gift. This type of existence in classical terms includes being open to the world, to the future, and to each other. All this is in contrast to being "curved within oneself," an apt description of sin and its effects. Still another way of speaking of the results of the gospel is in terms of the new person. In Christ I am new because Christ lives in me (Galatians 2:20).

Related to, and in some sense encompassing all the other effects is freedom. In the gospel of Jesus Christ we are free persons. We are free from any standard of acceptance other than God's, and he has accepted us in Christ. We are free from the law as a means of acceptance, free from death, now and in the future. We can be free from ourselves, from any legal or personal standards which we erect, from constant worry about how we feel. The significant fact is not how I feel, but the gracious words, "You are forgiven." We are free in a very positive sense from the evaluations of others, and need not even judge ourselves (1 Corinthians 4:2-5).

We are not only free *from,* but *to* and *for* something. Most importantly we are freed for a new life. "I have been crucified with Christ, it is no longer I who live, but Christ who lives in me; and the life I now live in the flesh I live by faith in the Son of God, who loved me and gave himself for me (Galatians 2:19-20). We are free for spontaneous, uncalculating service of others. As God relates to the believer without exchange, barter, or payment on our part, so the believer is freed to respond to the needs of others without calculating their worthiness or the expected return. We shall return to this theme when we consider the results of justification.

The Sacraments as Means of Grace

Melanchthon defined sacraments as "rites which have the command of God and to which the promise of grace has been added" (Apol. XIII, p. 211). The Word and the sacraments are correlatives for Lutheran theology, and both have as their content the gospel (A.C. VII, p. 32; XIV, p. 36; XXVIII, p. 82). The sacraments in this sense are only another form of the gospel, the good news of God's action in Christ and his intention for us. Sacraments, therefore, are not simply marks by which Christians are identified, "they are signs and testimonies of God's will toward us" (A.C. XIII, p. 35).

What distinguishes the sacraments from oral proclamation? First, the good news that is announced *in general* in preaching is applied *personally* in the sacraments. We are baptized and received into the believing community *by name*. In the Lord's Supper Christ is not only announced as present, but his body and blood, "are yours, as your treasure and gift" (L.C. V, 29, p. 449).

The words "for you" along with eating and drinking assure me that the sacrament is mine and is a blessing to me as "a sure sign and pledge" (L.C. V. 22, p. 449).

Second, in the sacraments the audible promise becomes a visible word, a "painting whereby the same is signified as is proclaimed through the Word" (Apol.

XIII, 5, p. 212). God has graciously moved to bring his gift in ways suited to our capacities, not only by the ear but also by our other senses. Thus through both Word and action he moves our hearts (Apol. XIII, 5, p. 212). This is what is meant when we speak of the sacraments as visible words of promise, enacted statements of grace.

Christian teaching regarding the number and nature of the sacraments has a long and varied history. By the time of the Reformation the Roman Catholic church, following a twelfth-century theologian, had agreed that there were seven acts in the church which deserved the title "sacrament." Lutherans, after considerable struggle, concluded that there were, in fact only two, or at most three sacraments, only three rites commanded by God to which a promise of grace had been added (Apol. XIII, p. 211). Baptism and the Lord's Supper were basic. Penitence was also suggested, but really fit under Baptism and was so considered.

Baptism

The Lutheran understanding of baptism is found in clearest form in the Augsburg Confession and the two catechisms. Baptism is a sacrament, a means by which God graciously initiates or incorporates one into a new relationship. It is the sign of a covenant relationship to which God always remains faithful, even in the face of unfaith. It is a means by which I am recalled again and again, and renewed in fellowship through daily repentance, which is nothing more than a return to one's baptismal covenant. The strongest defense found by Luther against the assaults of evil and the power of temptation was the reminder, "I have been baptized." Baptism is also the means by which we become priests before God, in the Reformation understanding.

124 The Means of Justification

How is it possible for the Confessors to make such glowing claims for this seemingly simple rite? What is so significant about this ceremony of initiation which has parallels in so many other religious bodies? Their answers concentrate on three themes: the need for baptism; the gifts of baptism; and the recipients of baptism (A.C. IX, p. 33).

The central place of baptism in the New Testament (Matthew 28:18; John 3:5; Romans 6:3) led the Reformers to assert that it was necessary for salvation (A.C. IX, 1, p. 33). This affirms that new birth, regeneration, and spiritual life are necessary and that these are given by God's loving action in baptism.

Questions sometimes arise, "What of those persons who die without baptism? Are they necessarily excluded? Are infants who die before receiving the sacrament necessarily lost?" The Roman Catholic tradition has spoken of an intermediary place where such unbaptized infants rest. It is called *limbo infantum*. Neither the Confessors nor the Scripture know of such a solution to the problem. We do know that God has directed and bound the church to baptize (L.C. IV, p. 440). Whether he has bound himself exclusively to this action we cannot say. The Word and sacraments are described as the "ordinary means or instruments" of God's gracious action (F.C.S.D. XI, p. 628).

Whether this leaves room for "extraordinary means" is left to his gracious decision. This type of position by no means allows the church to be casual about the sacrament. It is necessary: *we* are directed and bound to it. *Our* command is clear: it is to make disciples, baptizing and teaching. Whether God has bound himself to this means must be left open.

The gifts of baptism are the gifts of God's gracious action through the Word. The sacrament brings forgiveness, deliverance, and eternal salvation (S.C. IV, pp. 348-349). It signifies and effects regeneration and the death of the old man, that part of me which is opposed to the will and gracious intention of God (S.C. IV, p. 349; L.C., pp. 439-440). One is united with Christ and so led into, and equipped for new life in him (Romans 6:3 ff.).

As the Lutherans faced their Roman Catholic contemporaries, there was no great debate over the need and nature of baptism. As they looked in another direction, however, there was significant disagreement. Parts of the so-called left wing of the Reformation insisted that the sacrament, or ordinance as some of them called it, was properly limited to adults, or at least to those who had reached an age of accountability. This debate continues today between those who argue for and practice infant *and* adult baptism, and those who allow only adult participation.

This difference in practice often relates directly to the varying views of what baptism is. Some persons, for example, see the act as essentially following the example set by Jesus and his early followers; for others it is a public testimony of faith by the individual; still others describe it as a means of joining the church; and for some its meaning lies in the dedicating of children to God.

Each of these views emphasizes that baptism is basically something that *we* do. *I* follow, *I* bear witness, *I* join the church, or dedicate the children to God. The Confessors' stance is different. For them the center of a sacrament does not lie in what *I* do: it consists in *God's* action. Both baptism and the Lord's Supper are essentially God's action. My role is basically that of reception. The regular use of the passive form of the verb "to baptize" in the New Testament illustrates this. God is do-

ing something by this means; my part is basically acceptance.

What can be said in response to those who argue
against baptism of infants? You cannot assert that the
New Testament *explicitly* describes the baptism of infants. Certain assumptions may be made about "whole
households" being baptized (e.g., Acts 16:15, 33), but
there is no *specific* statement that infants were cared for
in this way.

If the argument from silence is not to be determina-
tive, other matters must also be considered. One of them
is the nature of sin and the need of the infant. If sin is
thought to be only an act in violation of a known command, then of course there is no need for baptism until
one is old enough to knowingly commit sin. There is no
need to baptize infants. If, on the other hand, sin is
understood not only as act, but also as a condition which
afflicts all, the question has a different context and answer. If all are involved, even the young, has God moved
to meet the needs that result from the condition? Baptism of the young is such an answer; it meets the need
of all.

The precedent of the Old Testament was sometimes
cited by the Reformers as a part of this debate. Colos-
sians 2:11-12 puts baptism and circumcision in parallel
positions. Baptism is described as circumcision not made
with hands. If the Apostle is correct in drawing the parallel, how far can we push the lines? What was the effect
of circumcision in the Old Covenant? It incorporated
one into the covenant people. When was it done, and
upon what profession of faith? It was done normally
when the boy was eight days old. There was, therefore,
obviously no personal confession of faith. If the parallel
holds, this is an argument for the inclusion of children
in baptism.

Luther and his colleagues also argued from their perception of history. The Western church had for centuries practiced the baptism of infants. If this were contrary to God's intention, there would have been no effect. But the church has survived, and many within it could be cited as living lives filled with the Spirit. This indicates that God was working through this means (L.C. p. 443).

A part of the opposition to infant baptism during the sixteenth century was tied to the concept, so central to Luther, of justification by grace through faith. If the gift of God in Jesus Christ must be received for its benefits to be known, and the means of reception is faith, then how can the gift in baptism be received by a person too young to have faith? Luther at times argued that infants do have faith, and it is a gift in them, just as in adults. At times he speaks of the faith of the believing congregation as of great importance in baptism. In the Confessions, however, he argues first, that the validity of baptism is not affected by our faith or lack of it (L.C. IV, p. 443). We baptize, with the purpose and hope that the child may believe, but solely on the basis of the command of God (p. 444).

The validity of baptism depends upon the Word of God rather than on faith. God has promised and tied himself to baptism. He establishes his covenant through this means and will remain true to it, even though I may fall away. It is the Word that is central. "My faith does not constitute baptism, but receives it" (p. 443).

The distinction between whether the sacrament is valid and whether its benefits are experienced is an important one. The validity depends upon God's Word and act; the experiencing of the benefits is through faith, through living the relationship established in the sacrament.

Baptism is for life, for living. My wife and I were married in 1951. Suppose the last time I saw her was on that same afternoon at the church. The marriage might be legal, lawful, and valid, but one might question whether a relationship really existed. Baptism is a sacrament of initiation, of beginnings. It inaugurates a new life in which one lives and grows. It is in this context that we talk about confession and repentance. What is confession? It is simply returning again and again to this relationship established in baptism. One can fall away, obviously, but God is faithful. He is always seeking me, and drawing me back to him, calling me to be what I am in Jesus Christ. The reality of life, and its continual amendment is called "using baptism" (p. 445). Repentance, in this context, is "really nothing else than baptism" (p. 445). "Repentance, therefore is nothing else than a return and approach to Baptism, to resume and practice what had earlier been begun but abandoned" (p. 446).

It is in faith, itself a gift from God, that one experiences the benefits of baptism. It is as we "travel wet" from the water of baptism that we live in the new relationship of daily repentance and forgiveness.

The Lord's Supper

The Confessors faced in two directions as they presented their understanding of the Lord's Supper. As they dealt with their Roman Catholic contemporaries, the issues centered on whether the sacrament could in any sense be seen as a meritorious sacrifice, whether it was necessary and proper to use the doctrine of transubstantiation to explain the presence of Christ in the Supper, and whether it was correct to withhold the cup from the laity. The first of these concerns was by far the most significant in their view.

As they faced the Zwinglians and some others, the debate centered on whether it was appropriate to affirm that the risen Christ was really present in the sacrament, whether the memorial aspect of the Supper was being properly dealt with, and whether it was correct to maintain that the risen Christ was now at the right hand of the Father, if this was taken as a spatial designation.

The central issue in the entire discussion is the real presence of the body and blood of Christ in the Sacrament, and what this does and does not mean. Although the Confessions are written by different persons and are spread over many years, there is a remarkable consistency on the doctrine of the real presence. Their conviction that the risen Christ was present among his people by means of the sacrament was based on a particular understanding of the New Testament and was shared by Roman Catholics and Eastern Christians.

In opposition to any attempt to explain *how* the presence could be affirmed, the Confessors refer to the real presence "with" the visible elements (Apol. X, pp. 179-180), "under the form of bread and wine" (A.C. X, p. 34; S.C. p. 351), "in and under" (L.C., p. 447), and "under the bread, with the bread, in the bread" (F.C.S.D. VII, 35, 37ff., p. 575). If Christ has promised to be present "for us" by these particular means, there is no need to rationally demonstrate its possibility; all that is needed is trust in his promise and obedience to his command. One bows before and embraces the mystery.

On the other flank of the controversy, the Confessors faced those who denied Christ's presence in the Supper, except in faith, since he was thought to be limited in space to the "right hand of God." In response, the Lutherans argued that the opponents' symbolic interpre-

tation of the words of institution denied the clear meaning of the text, that their limitation of the risen Christ
to a particular place was based on an inadequate Christology that ignored the "personal union" of the divine
and human in him, and misunderstood the phrase the
"right hand of God" (F.C.S.D. VII, p. 587; VIII, 17, p.
594). The basic texts, they argued, assert Christ's presence. As risen and glorified, he is everywhere present,
and present in the sacrament in a saving manner, "for
us" according to his promise. The "right hand of God,"
as used in the Scriptures and the creeds, denotes that all
power is his, not that he is limited to a particular space
(F.C.S.D. VIII, p. 596).

The most the Confessors wish to say is that by means
of what they call a "sacramental union" Christ is present
in, with, and under the consecrated elements and is active for us in a saving manner (F.C.S.D. VII, 37, p. 575).
We insist *that* he is present; to say *how* exceeds our abilities, for Christ's words, "This is my body," are an absolutely unique expression (F.C.S.D. VII, 38, p. 578).

What kind of eating and drinking occur in the sacrament? The Confessors insist that it is precisely *in* the
eating and drinking that the Lord's body and blood and
their effects come to us (S.C. VI, p. 352).

There is a double aspect to this eating. One is spiritual. This is precisely faith, "namely, that we hear, accept with faith and appropriate to ourselves the Word
of God, in which Christ, true God and man, together
with all his benefits . . . is presented" (F.C.S.D. VII, 61-
63, p. 580). The other eating is "oral or sacramental,"

> when all who eat and drink the blessed bread and wine
> in the Lord's Supper receive and partake of the true,
> essential body and blood of Christ orally. Believers
> receive it as a certain pledge and assurance that their

sins are truly forgiven, that Christ dwells and is efficacious in them; unbelievers receive it orally too, but
to their judgment and damnation *(Ibid.)*.

The Confessors wished to stand against the opponents
in asserting the reality of Christ's saving presence, while
denying the attacks that accused them of transubstantiation, cannibalism, or "capernaitic eating . . . as though
one rent Christ's flesh with one's teeth and digested it
like other food" (F.C.Ep. VII, 42, p. 486). Rather the
eating is done "spiritually," by "the spiritual, supernatu-
ral, heavenly mode according to which Christ is present
in the Holy Supper, not only to work comfort in believers, but also to wreak judgment on unbelievers"
(F.C.S.D. VII, 105, p. 588).

The Confessions refer to the adverse effects of the sacrament on unbelievers. It was possible to partake "unworthily," not discerning the body (1 Corinthians
11:29). Whether the "body" in this passage refers to
Christ's presence among his people by means of the bread
and wine, or to the presence of his "body, the church" is
debated by some today. In either instance it is possible,
according to Paul, to partake unworthily.

This is certainly not a reference to moral worthiness in
which one becomes "good enough" to take the sacrament. This old view, often common among Scandinavian
Lutherans, has been a source of considerable distress.
The Supper is precisely for those who are unworthy sinners. True worthiness is summarized: "He is truly worthy
and well prepared who believes these words: 'for you'
and 'for the forgiveness of sins' " (S.C. VI, 10, p. 352).

The richness of the gifts and nature of the sacrament
defy description, but certain themes are evident in the
Confessions. For one thing the sacrament is to be understood as a gift given by God. Christ himself "offers us all

the treasure he brought from heaven for us" (L.C. V, 66, p. 454). He is here to forgive, to save, to share, to unite, to strengthen, to give life and comfort (L.C. V, 22, p. 449).

The sacrament is also "a true bond or union of Christians with Christ their head and with one another" (F.C.S.D. VII, 44, p. 577). This union is not essentially one of action, but of receiving. The communion or sharing with Christ results in sharing, participation in the mutual love of the brethren.

The sacrament is also a remembrance. The Lord had instructed his people, "to do this in remembrance." By this he intended that this act should be "an abiding memorial of his bitter passion and death, and of all his blessings" *(Ibid.)*. What is this "remembrance of Christ"? It is "the remembrance of Christ's blessings and the acceptance of them by faith, so that they make us alive" (Apol. XXIV, 71, p. 262). It is faith that remembers "what benefits are received through Christ . . . which cheer and comfort anxious consciences" (A.C. IV, 30, p. 59).

The Holy Supper is also understood in terms of sacrifice. Here the Roman Catholic position, as understood by the Confessors, is carefully avoided by means of a distinction between what they term "propitiatory" and "eucharistic" sacrifices. The first reconciles God and merits forgiveness for others; the second is simply a means by which those already reconciled by God give thanks or show their gratitude (Apol. XXIV, 19, p. 252). There has been only one propitiatory sacrifice, that of Christ himself. We do offer sacrifices of praise and thanksgiving. This last note of eucharist, or thanksgiving, provides another crucial dimension to an understanding of the sacrament. Confronted by the magnitude of Christ's saving work here presented in the Holy Supper, the believer responds and "uses the ceremony itself as praise to God, as a demonstration of gratitude, and as a witness of its high esteem for God's gifts. . . . Thus the ceremony becomes a sacrifice of praise" (Apol. XXIV, 74, p. 263; cf. also 356, 87-88, 93) .

The Supper is God's gift, to be received in faith. In it the dimensions of communion, memorial, sacrifice, and thanksgiving all have appropriate places. It effects the same reconciliation and fellowship as the proclaimed Word. Its benefits are summarized by the words, forgiveness of sins, life, and salvation. For where there is forgiveness of sins there are life and salvation (S.C. VI, p. 352; cf. also L.C. V, p. 454) .

As long as these central themes are kept clear and maintained, that is, as long as the gracious word of the gospel is not confused, the Confessors were willing to allow wide latitude in expression and practice. No rules were made regarding rites and ceremonies, as long as the central focus remained undisturbed and unclouded (A.C. VII, p. 32; A.C. XV, p. 36) .

The center of the Confessions is justification by grace through faith. Its basis is the sheer unutterable love of God, seen in Jesus Christ, made known and applied to us by the Holy Spirit. It is needed because of our desperate situation "in the presence of God"—that is, because of the seriousness of sin. God has chosen to use particular external means to bring his saving message. These are the church, the ministry, and the means of grace. In every instance the reference point and the central message concerns the loving Father who is at work to reconcile and sustain his children.

7 The Results of Justification

With the addition of this chapter our circular diagram becomes complete. Review once again its form:

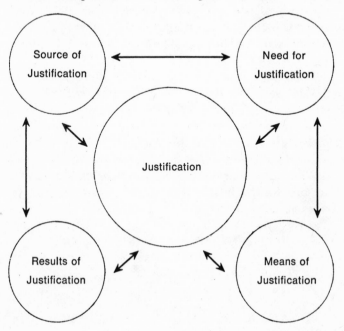

Our discussion of the Christian life as described in the Confessions will be based on the materials noted in the new circle.

Results of
Justification
A.C. & Apol. VI,
XVI, XX
S.A. III, 13
F.C. IV
S.C. & L.C. 346-348,
420-436, 352-356

If God, because of his love, has moved to reconcile the enemy, bring back the lost, to justify sinners through the life and work of Christ as mediated to the world by external means he has chosen, the question remains, "So what?" To what end has fellowship been reestablished? What are the characteristics of Christian life in and for the world?

These questions all relate to what is sometimes called sanctification. They raise particular problems for Lutherans, for we have often been so concerned with describing *how* one is received into relationship that we seem almost out of breath when it comes to describing what life in this new context is like. This issue, of course, was not one of great controversy in the sixteenth century. It is therefore not addressed with the same attention and passion as are some others. The Tappert edition of the Book of Concord, for example, has 636 pages of text; only 36 deal specifically with sanctification. But there is a constant danger of emphasizing justification to the point where we exclude concern for the Christian life, of separating profession from life, and faith from action. Our basic question, therefore, is: what follows justification, acceptance, reconciliation "because of Christ, through faith"?

Biblical Pictures of the Life of Faith

The Scriptures emphasize what it means to be a member of a covenant people, who have been received into relationship by grace. Two things are clear: first, one does not move into fellowship with God by performance of law, by being good, but rather by God's sovereign and gracious choice and action. This is the point of Paul's emphasis on how long after the covenant was established that the law was given (Galatians 3:17).

Second, a certain type of life was expected among this covenant people. Faith and life, profession and practice, were somehow expected to hang together. They were to constitute a coherent whole. The prophets spoke with great passion against those who did not bring together their religious life, characterized by cultic observances, and their everyday activities. Listen, for example to Isaiah:

Hear the word of the Lord,
　you rulers of Sodom!
Give ear to the teaching of our God,
　you people of Gomorrah!
"What to me is the multitude of your sacrifices?"
　says the Lord;
"I have had enough of burnt offerings of rams
　and the fat of fed beasts;
I do not delight in the blood of bulls,
　or of lambs, or of he-goats.

"When you come to appear before me,
　who requires of you this trampling of my courts?
Bring no more vain offerings;
　incense is an abomination to me.
New moon and sabbath and the calling of assemblies—

I cannot endure iniquity and solemn assembly. . . .
Wash yourselves; make yourselves clean;
   remove the evil of your doings
   from before my eyes;
cease to do evil,
   learn to do good;
seek justice,
   correct oppression;
defend the fatherless,
   plead for the widow" (1:10-13, 16, 17).

In the prophet Amos the same dichotomy of faith and life brings the same judgment:

I hate, I despise your feasts,
   and I take no delight in your solemn assemblies.
Even though you offer me your burnt offerings and
   cereal offerings,
   I will not accept them,
and the peace offerings of your fatted beasts
   I will not look upon.
Take away from me the noise of your songs;
   to the melody of your harps I will not listen.
But let justice roll down like waters,
   and righteousness like an ever-flowing stream
(5:21-24) .

This same theme runs throughout the New Testament. Our Lord always speaks of the continuing mercy of God, yet notes with both sorrow and anger a falling away in faith and in life. There is a contradiction between profession and practice. At one point, for example, he described the religious leaders, those who had authority in the community:

The scribes and the Pharisees sit on Moses' seat; so practice and observe whatever they tell you, but not what they do; for they preach, but do not practice. They bind heavy burdens, hard to bear, and lay them on men's shoulders; but they themselves will not move them with their finger. They do all their deeds to be seen by men (Matthew 23:2-5).

The letters of the New Testament community are also instructive. We may learn, not only from what they say, but also from the very form they adopt. St. Paul, for example, in Romans, begins with the theological dimension, demonstrating in the first chapters the basic sinfulness and need of all persons. No one is righteous before God, "But now the righteousness of God has been manifested apart from law, although the law and prophets bear witness to it, the righteousness of God through faith in Jesus Christ for all who believe" (3:21). He illustrates this by the life of Abraham, and speaks of the peace and joy and hope and love which God has given (Chapters 4 and 5). The theological discussion and argumentation continue, all pointing to the sovereign, gracious act of God and what this means. And then—the great *therefore*. "Therefore . . . present your bodies as a living sacrifice, holy and acceptable to God (12:1). You have seen what God is and does, what he did and is doing, *therefore* present yourselves to him.

The same pattern is found in Galatians. We begin with what God has graciously done, and then in Chapter 5, the conclusion: "For freedom Christ has set us free; stand fast therefore, and do not submit again to a yoke of slavery" (Galatians 5:1). The call is that we *be* what we *are* in Christ.

The Christian Life: A Lutheran View

The Confessors do not ignore this motif, but express it quite simply and directly with the words: "It is also taught among us that such faith should produce good fruits and good works and that we must do all such good works as God has commanded, but we should do them for God's sake and not place our trust in them as if thereby to merit favor before God" (A.C. VI, pp. 31-32).

In this discussion the same distinction between life "in the presence of men" and "in the presence of God" must be maintained in order to understand the Confessors. It is certainly possible for any person to do good works in a civil sense. To endow a hospital is good work whether done by a Christian or a non-believer. Good works "in the presence of men" are required by God; they are to be praised and even rewarded (Apol. IV, p. 110). Since faith, however, is the prerequisite for entrance into life "in the presence of God," good works in this context only spring from relationship already established. They do not cause or establish it.

There is an interesting and helpful connection between Articles IV, V, and VI of the Augsburg Confession. Article IV asserts that we are justified by God, "freely, because of Christ, through faith." Article V maintains that in order that "this faith may be obtained" God instituted the office of the ministry. What faith? The faith which apprehends and clings to what God has done in Christ; the faith through which we are justified. Article VI continues that such faith will produce good fruits. Again, what faith? It is justifying faith which is obtained through Word and sacraments, and which clings to its object, Jesus Christ. Not just any faith will produce good fruits "in the presence of God." The Confessors are saying

> that if you truly believe God loves you and all other men unconditionally, a life of love and service will result. If you really believe that your sins are for-

given, you are enabled to forgive those who have of-
fended and hurt you. This method is not the way we
train animals; if you want to teach a dog a trick, you
reward him after he has rolled over, stood on his hind
legs, or barked. If you give him his dog-candy first, he
will not do a thing. The Augsburg Confession claims
that God treats us like men, not like dogs, forgives us
our sins, and shows us his love first, and expects us
then to forgive and show love to others.[1]

The goal of justification or its synonyms, therefore, is
not simply a new status, but a new life; not simply a
new attitude, or state of mind, but a new action; not
simply a new situation, but a new person. God has acted
so that I may "thank, praise, serve, and obey him" (S.C.
p. 345). Christ works, "so that I may live under him in
his kingdom, and serve him in everlasting righteousness,
innocence, and blessedness" *(Ibid.)*. And this is not put
off to someday, somewhere else. The new age has already
broken in upon us in Christ; this is the time of the new
life of service and love.

What is this faith like, and what does it do? Luther
describes it, characteristically, in very energetic terms:

Faith is a divine work in us that transforms us and
begets us anew from God, kills the Old Adam, makes
us entirely different people in heart, spirit, mind, and
all our powers, and brings the Holy Spirit with it. Oh,
faith is a living, busy, active, mighty thing, so that it is
impossible for it not to be constantly doing what is
good. Likewise, faith does not ask if good works are to
be done, but before one can ask, faith has already
done them and is constantly active. Whoever does not
perform such good works is a faithless man, blindly
tapping around in search of faith and good works
without knowing what either faith or good works are,

and in the meantime he chatters and jabbers a great
deal about faith and good works. Faith is a vital, de-
liberate trust in God's grace, so certain that it would
die a thousand times for it. And such confidence and
knowledge of divine grace makes us joyous, mettle-
some, and merry toward God and all creatures. This
the Holy Spirit works by faith, and therefore without
any coercion a man is willing and desirous to do good
to everyone. . . . It is therefore as impossible to separate works from faith as it is to separate heat and
light from fire (F.C.S.D. IV, pp. 552-553).

As a divine action faith transforms, brings a new birth
and the Holy Spirit. The effect of faith in my life is that
I am busy and active, doing good. I am now joyous,
bold, and full of life. And I now am able to do good
through the Spirit spontaneously, without being coerced.
The type of Christian who feels the only appropriate
attitude for the person of faith is one of constant sorrow
and gloom might well consider the description offered by
the Reformer.

The statements on "The New Obedience" can be understood best in their historical context. The position
taken directly opposes two other views that were current
at the time. One might argue that they persist to our
own day, perhaps in slightly different form. If this is
true then Article VI continues to be relevant.

On the one hand the Confessors oppose those of their
contemporaries who held that a person could rely upon
works in some sense in the establishment and main-
tenance of relationship "in the presence of God." This
approach is in error because it makes the effect into a
cause; it puts the cart before the horse. Since the Confessors had established, to their own satisfaction, that
both the Scriptures and experience show that one is ac-

cepted by God *only* through his grace, without works, it is useless to reintroduce works as a means of new life now that we are talking about what it means to be Christian. Luther's own experience of despair at the demand that "one do what lies within him" in order to be received by God was also influential in establishing the position.

On the other hand, some people argued that since one is saved by faith, no real amendment of life is necessary for the Christian. These persons, sometimes called "libertines" by their opponents, held that one should live as he pleased. The separation of profession and practice contributed to a chaotic situation in which "each man did what was right in his own eyes" (Judges 21:25).

Works are the result, not the cause, of the new relationship. The indispensable ingredient in any concept of Christian living is faith which is itself a gift of God. It is the Holy Spirit who "calls, gathers, enlightens and sanctifies" (S.C., p. 345). Sanctification is the characteristic of the Christian life. It is only through the Spirit that one can do works that are pleasing "in the presence of God" (A.C. XX, pp. 45-46).

"Whenever good works are praised and the law preached, therefore, we must hold fast to these rules: that the law is not kept without Christ—as he himself has said, 'Apart from me you can do nothing' (John 15:5) —and that 'without faith it is impossible to please God' " (Hebrews 11:6; Apol. IV, p. 147).

It may not be argued that faith in Christ initiates relationship and that then my own good efforts take over to maintain it. Everything is tied to continued faithfulness. "In other words, St. Paul attributes to faith alone the beginning, the middle, and the end of everything" (F.C.S.D. IV, p. 556).

Our continuing tendency toward legalism, toward trying to establish some means or action to which God must respond favorably, to enter into a theology of barter or of the market place, makes the Confessions' warnings about the danger of relying on works most helpful. To place our trust, even in the smallest way, in our own efforts "in the presence of God" obscures the glory of Christ by placing our achievements alongside his. This brings no peace of conscience, notably in times of stress, for there is no assurance that one has ever done enough. Finally this course denies one any sure knowledge of what God is like. He is always seen as demanding more than we can do, and as a result one is always angry and running away (Apol. IV, p. 135; cf. also Apol. XX, p. 227).

Everything indeed is from the hand of God, who gives because of his gracious love and our need. When we have believed all, and done all, we still can only say, "We are unprofitable servants; we have only done what was our duty" (Luke 17:10; cf. A.C. VI, p. 32).

Why Faithful Works Are to Be Done

If we are accepted by God "because of Christ, through faith," why then should we be concerned about works, about a style of life at all? Works are necessary for at least four reasons, according to the Confessors:

1. because God has commanded them

2. because they are a means by which we exercise faith

3. because they enable us to give testimony

4. because they are means by which we render thanks (Apol. IV, p. 133).

Good works spring from faith and correspond to God's intention for his people. In the Scriptures it is written,

"For we are his workmanship, created in Christ Jesus for good works which God prepared beforehand that we should walk in them" (Ephesians 2:10).

In such activity God "sanctifies hearts and suppresses the devil" (Apol. IV, p. 133). Good works are "the outward administration of Christ's rule among men" *(Ibid.)*. In this context the Confessors have only positive things to say. Such works are done because God has commanded them.

The Christian does good works as an exercise of faith. Here the athletic imagery so significant in St. Paul is important. The Christian does "fight the good fight of faith"; he does run the course, and train as an athlete for an "incorruptible prize" (1 Timothy 6:12; 2 Timothy 4:7-8; Ephesians 6:10ff.). The Epistle of James suggests that faith without life, that is, without works is dead. It is not faith at all (James 2:14ff.). Luther's insistence that faith itself is busy, active, constantly at work adds color to the picture. Works, in the Christian, are seen as a sign of the existence of faith. "For when good works are done on account of right causes and for the right ends (that is, with the intention that God demands of the regenerated), they are an indication of salvation in believers" (Philippians 1:28; F.C.S.D. IV, p. 557). Since the existence of faith itself cannot be empirically demonstrated, the best that works can supply are clues to the fact that God is in fact active.

The intimate, indissoluble relation between faith, love, and the Christian life is clearly put by Luther in several writings. At one point he faced the problem of some of his followers who wished to establish the Reformation by legal means, rather than by the persuasion of preaching the gospel. This happened in Wittenberg while Luther was absent. When he returned, he preached eight sermons which stopped this type of reform. In this context he wrote:

There must also be love. And through love we must do unto one another what God has done unto us through faith. For without love, faith is nothing; as St. Paul says in 1 Corinthians, "If I speak with the tongues of angels and do the highest things of faith, but have not love, I am nothing." And here, dear friends, have you not grievously failed? I see no signs of love among you. And I observe that you have not been grateful to God for his rich gifts and treasures. Let us beware lest Wittenberg become Capernaum. I notice that you have a great deal to say of the doctrine which is preached to you of faith and of love. This is not surprising. An ass can almost intone the lessons. And why should you not be able to repeat the doctrines and formulas. Dear friends, the kingdom of God, as we are that kingdom, consists not in speech nor in words, but in deeds, in works, in exercises. God does not want hearers and repeaters of words, but doers and followers who exercise themselves in the faith that works by love, for a faith without love is not enough, for it is not faith at all, but a counterfeit faith, just as a face seen in a mirror is not a real face, but merely the reflection of the face.[2]

The Christian life is a means of giving testimony, of making a confession of faith. While it may be argued that in a real sense it is not possible to differentiate kind, altruistic works done by the believer and the non-believer, there is, I believe, a basic difference in motivation and in power. We are exhorted in the New Testament to live our lives in a particular way, to do our work for particular reasons. One does not light a candle and put it under a cover, but rather on a candlestick;

one does not try to hide a city that is set on a hill. The conclusion of these simple comparisons made by our Lord is, "Let your light so shine before men, that they may see your good works and give glory to your father who is in heaven" (Matthew 5:16). Good works, in the view of the Confessors, do give testimony; they bear witness.

Finally, the Christian life is a way to render thanks. Good works are a joyful response to the goodness of God. They are an expression of the sacrificial dimension of Christian experience (Romans 12:1; Hebrews 13:15). According to the Confessions good works include "sacrifices of praise; the proclamation of the Gospel, faith, prayer, thanksgiving, confession, the afflictions of the saints, yes, all the good works of the saints" (Apol. XXIV, 25, p. 253).

To whom, and in what way is such thanks given? Since God is the giver our grateful response should go to him. But what does God need from us? His glory is not diminished without our praise; his power is not lessened without our gifts. Even if all the world should say no, he is God and thus is always the giver, not the dependent receiver. Where and to whom can our thanks be given? To the neighbor—to those around us. For it is precisely in the needs and anguish of "one of the least of these" that we meet Christ and serve the king (Matthew 25:31ff.). The fruit of the gospel, whether preached or received in the sacraments, is love, and love expresses itself to the neighbor. This theme is often found in Luther. At one point he writes,

> We now speak of the fruit of this sacrament, which is love; that is, that we treat our neighbor even as God has treated us. Now, we have received from God nothing but love and favor, for Christ has pledged and

given us his righteousness and everything that he is, has poured out upon us all his treasures, which no man can measure and no angel can understand or fathom, for God is a glowing furnace of love, reaching even from the earth to the heavens. Love, I say, is the fruit of the sacrament. But I do not yet perceive it among you here in Wittenberg. Although there is much preaching of love and you ought to practice it in all things. This is the principle thing and alone is seemly in a Christian. But no one shows eagerness for this, and you want to do all sorts of unnecessary things, which are of no account. If you do not want to show yourselves Christians by your love, then leave the other things undone, too.[3]

We render thanks to God by lives of love which focus on our neighbor.

If someone asks, "Are the Lutherans concerned about good works and the Christian life?" the answer is, "Yes, but we understand them to be the result rather than the cause of relationship." If the questioning goes on: "Why should one do them?" the Confessors' answer: "We do them because God has commanded them, to exercise our faith, to give testimony, and to render thanks."

Perceptive persons are often not content simply to look at a deed itself and its effects; they wish to ask further questions that probe into the motivations behind an act. What is it that moves an individual to a particular style of life and form of action? Two themes present themselves: one points to an inner drive, the other to an outer force. In the Lutheran Confessions the emphasis is on the inner drive.

It is the gospel itself that moves the Christian to action. The words "I have redeemed you . . . I have loved you with an everlasting love" cannot be ignored by the

believer. Our Lord encourages and impels the believer
with the words, "I chose you and appointed you that
you should go and bear fruit and that your fruit should
abide" (John 15:16). Paul speaks about how the "love of
Christ controls us" (2 Corinthians 5:14). There is an
inner drive—a compulsion, if you will—to move, to act.
Once again the central issue is the relationship between
faith and love, between love received and love expressed.
In the treatise *On Christian Liberty,* sometimes called
The Freedom of the Christian, Luther puts it clearly:

> Thus from faith flow forth love and joy in the Lord,
> and from the Lord, love, a joyful willing and free
> mind that serves the neighbor willingly and takes no
> account of gratitude or ingratitude, of praise or blame,
> of gain or loss. . . . Hence as our heavenly Father has
> in Christ freely come to our help, we also ought freely
> to help our neighbor through our body and its works,
> and each should become as it were a Christ to the
> other, that we may be Christs to one another and
> Christ may be the same in all; that is, that we may be
> truly Christians. Who then can comprehend the riches
> and glory of the Christian life? It can do all things,
> and has all things, and lacks nothing; it is lord over
> sin, death and hell, and yet at the same time it serves,
> ministers to and benefits all men. . . . Surely we are so
> named after Christ, not because He is absent from us,
> but because He dwells in us, that is, because we be-
> lieve on Him and are Christs one to another and do
> to our neighbors as Christ does to us.[4]

In another place Luther notes,

> The Christian man lives not in himself, but in Christ
> and in his neighbor. Otherwise he is not a Christian.
> He lives in Christ through faith, in his neighbor

through love; by faith he is caught up beyond himself into God, by love he sinks down beneath himself into his neighbor; yet he always remains in God and in His love.[5]

There is this inner drive, this compulsion to actions which are uncalculating and spontaneous, which moves one to serve even in adversity. One may be sure that this type of life will not be an endless parade of joyous and victorious moments.

For where God's Word is preached, accepted or believed, and bears fruit, there the blessed holy cross will not be far away. Let nobody think that he will have peace; he must sacrifice all he has on earth—possessions, honor, house and home, wife and children, body and life. Now, this grieves our flesh and the old Adam, for it means that we must remain steadfast, suffer patiently whatever befalls us, and let go whatever is taken from us (L.C., p. 429).

There is joy even in adversity, service even in suffering. We are moved and called to this by an inner drive, "not from a fear of punishment, like a slave, but out of a love of righteousness, like a child" (F.C. Ep. IV, p. 477).

While the actions of the Christian on behalf of the neighbor, and the effects of such action, may not always be distinguished from those of the altruistic, philanthropic non-believer, there is a difference in motivation and in power. A few years ago I attended a meeting where one of the main speakers was a lawyer who specialized in representing slum-dwellers bringing action against their landlords. The lawyer was poorly paid, but dedicated to his work. We pictured him as one of God's noblemen. He was doing a good thing, something that had to be done. I asked him how he got into this work, and why he stayed in it, expecting an answer about how he loved these poor people and wanted to help them. On the contrary, his answer was simply, "I hate those bastard slum lords." As it developed, he had no respect or affection for his clients. His hatred was all that carried him along. I wondered at the time how long he could remain in the work. He is not doing it now. I have never known anyone who could continue a great length of time to operate purely on the basis of hate. Hatred passes—but love, as Paul understood so well, never ends. Life that finds its motivation in an awareness of the continuing inexhaustible love of God, finds a motivation and a power that does not end.

A second motivational factor is, by contrast, one of outward drive and, if you will, compulsion. Concerned about some who leaned toward antinomianism, the Confessors insisted that good works are also a result of the law. The old man still exists and must be pushed to responsible action. The spontaneity of loving action is not perfect, even among the children of God; we are still encumbered with weakness, "as St. Paul complains of himself in Romans 7:14-25 and Galatians 5:17" (F.C. Ep. IV, p. 477).

The obedience of love is desired, but our coolness and indifference also bring the law into play. This moves us to action, and also drives us back to Christ, that is to a relationship where we see again "that our works should be done, not that we may be justified by them; since being justified beforehand by faith, we ought to do all things faithfully and joyfully for the sake of others." [6]

In summary, the life of the Christian in the world, has a number of significant dimensions.

It is a life of *freedom*. Freedom from law and wrath— we are loved; freedom from the fear of death—we already have the new life; freedom from rejection—we are already accepted. We are also free for service to others in spontaneous, uncalculating action.

The Christian life is also characterized by *creativity*. Genuine, authentic existence is constructive as we participate in God's continuing creative process in our vocations. Our labor is not a punishment for being human; it is a part of God's sustaining and transforming of the world.

The Christian life is one of *illumination*. Life, in the context of Christ, is seen as what it is meant to be, that is, a mutual ministering of love. This insight is a source of both joy, and frustration as our aspirations for loving action are hindered by the continuing fact of evil. It is also a persistent and powerful motive to action in and for the world.

The life in Christ is also one of *power*. In the Holy Spirit there is power to achieve and actualize newness. A share in this power is an essential part of the Christian life and action. While we do not yet have the fullness of that for which we wait, we do have the "earnest money," the down payment that indicates that what is promised, that is, the resurrection when all will be new, is indeed coming (Ephesians 1:13-14).

The Christian life, although marred by sin, is marked by constructive, powerful, informed, and creative desire to share all good things, all of God's gifts with others. This is in grateful response to what has already been done for and to us. It is a response to God's love that is directed in spontaneous and uncalculating acts of service to others. The attitude of being "a Christ to the other" continues to this day to characterize those who are "in Christ."

Epilog: The Lutheran Confessions in Our Lives Today

An old teacher of mine used to punctuate his lectures with the words, "Enough of that, on to the next point." While we could hardly claim to have had "enough" of our subject, if that were to mean we have dealt with it fully and well, it is perhaps time to move on. It is time to move beyond study and analysis into application and life. Just as a liturgy is meant to be prayed and not dissected, so a confession of faith is meant to be confessed and lived, not simply studied.

One last remaining look at the ground we have covered might be appropriate. The themes and even the words of our study may help us move on.

The basic question for the Reformers was always focused on how one is received into relationship with God. If we are made for fellowship with God and each other, our lives cannot be complete and full unless these personal relationships exist. When we are alone and alienated from our Creator and from those around us, we are like eagles, made for the wide skies who now perch in a cage, or like sailors born and bred to the heave of a deck and the sting of salt spray who now sit ashore watching their rusting ships. We are made for better things than enmity and fear and hostility. Our hearts are restless, as Augustine put it, until they find their rest in God.

If we are made for fellowship and exist more fully and completely within this context, what can we do to enter it? Nothing at all. The effects of evil in the world and in each of us are so disastrous that of ourselves we have neither the ability nor the inclination to establish the ties with God and our neighbors.

Does this leave us with only an occasional wistful yearning for better things, but with no hope of attaining them? Will we always be striving, but never obtaining? Always reaching, but never arriving?

No. We can hope, obtain, and arrive. Not, however, by the path we choose—but by the route that is given by God. As we look at ourselves there is only enmity, hostility, and guilt. But as our eyes are drawn to Another, we find all that was meant to be, for "all the promises of God find their Yes in him" (2 Corinthians 1:20).

The vision of the believer is always focused on the figure of Jesus Christ who comes to us by the Spirit. In this wondrous man we meet God himself, the God who creates, sustains, and loves what he has made, forever. There is nothing that we can say, or do, or be that can stop God from loving us. And in Christ, he has given us himself, withholding nothing (L.C. p. 413).

How do we receive this incomparable gift, this unbelievable promise? Simply by trusting the giver, by believing the promiser. If we believe him, he and all that he is—is ours.

What then—or is this the end of it all?

We must say another word, for life *within* the relationship is also of crucial importance. Faith has substance and form. It clings and entrusts itself to Another and at the same time it motivates and empowers to a new life. While we meet and *believe* the Lord who comes to us in the Word, the sacraments, and in the church, we meet and *serve* him as he comes to us in the needs of our neighbor and of the world. We are now free persons— free to love, to serve, even to die, and thus to live, just as he has done and continues to do for us.

This message of faith and freedom is what has been given us. It is what we offer to others.

One way in which we are guided and informed in our receiving for ourselves and our offering of this gift of the gospel to others is by the constructive use of the confessional writings. These documents are not judicial statements that bind us in a legal way to the past. They do not provide a series of all-encompassing and all-reliable rules for faith and conduct. On the other hand, they are not simply historical artifacts—curios of a bygone era.

Rather they describe, protect, and offer the treasure of a particular understanding of the Christian tradition to our day. In this they help hold us to the center of the message and always point to the gospel—to Christ. The Confessions sometimes reflect battles which are no longer appropriate; they occasionally use language which obscures rather than clarifies for our day; their exegesis of the Scriptures is sometimes in error. We grant all these— but at the same time argue that the statements are of inestimable value to us today. Why? Because for all their time-conditionedness, for all their ancient battles and awkward formulations, they do understand and clearly present one crucial thing—the gospel.

Again and again, without fail, without hesitation they return to the center. By doing this they call us to attend, to listen, not to themselves but to the gospel. Thus they lead us to the freedom which is only to be found in Christ.

We need this leading, this reminding, for while we were made for fellowship and for the freedom of faith, left alone we always turn to plans of pride which turn us in upon ourselves, to bondage. How many schemes do good religious persons create to please and placate God? How many dreams and devices are created to make us acceptable to God? Am I good enough, pious enough, intelligent enough, humble enough? Is not the path I choose to walk one of righteousness? Must not God, therefore, be pleased and accepting?

The Confessors, because they understand both legalism and the gospel, say no to such questions and to such plans. All the religious systems of mankind share the notion that God does business with good people; they may not be perfect but they have done their best. Only the gospel, this good news which transcends all our plans, understands that *God does business with sinners*. Fellowship and new life are offered to sinners who receive them only by faith. They eventuate in freedom which makes all things new and leads us into a future that belongs to God.

It is to such a life and such a future of faith and freedom that the Lutheran Confessions would lead us.

Notes

CHAPTER 2. THE NEED FOR CONFESSIONAL WRITINGS

1. *Luther's Works.* American Edition. Vol. 22. (St. Louis: Concordia Publishing House, 1957) , pp. 105-106.

CHAPTER 3. JUSTIFICATION: THE CENTER OF THE LUTHERAN CONFESSIONS

1. See Gerhard Kittel, *Theological Dictionary of the New Testament* tr. by Geoffrey W. Bromiley (Grand Rapids: Eerdmans Publishing Company, 1967) , pp. 176-229. Also Exod. 23:7; Prov. 17:15; Matt. 12:37).
2. Canons and Decrees of the Sacred and Oecumenical Council of Trent. tr. J. Waterworth (Chicago: Christian Symbolical Pub. Soc., n.d.) Canon XI.
3. See his *Lecture Notes on Romans,* ed. W. Pauck (Philadelphia: Westminster, 1961) , pp. 120ff., 125, 204 f., 322.
4. For a helpful summary see Gustav Aulen, *Christus Victor* tr. by A. G. Hebert (New York: MacMillan & Co., 1951) .
5. Werner Elert, *The Structure of Lutheranism* (St. Louis: Concordia, 1962) , p. 104.
6. See *Luther's Works.* American Edition. Vol. 34, (Philadelphia: Fortress, 1960) , pp. 110-11.
7. *Ibid.,* Vol. 44, p. 23.
8. *Ibid.,* Vol. 31, p. 357.
9. For illustrative material on this theme, see my *The Reformation Then and Now* (Minneapolis: Augsburg, 1966) , pp. 34ff.

CHAPTER 4. THE SOURCE OF JUSTIFICATION

1. E. Schlink, *Theology of the Lutheran Confessions* (Philadelphia: Muhlenberg, 1961), p. 51.
2. See H. E. Jacobs, *A Summary of the Christian Faith* (Philadelphia: United Lutheran Publishing House, 1905), pp. 159-193.

CHAPTER 5. THE NEED FOR JUSTIFICATION

1. See Reinhold Niebuhr, *The Nature and Destiny of Men* (New York: Scribners, 1955), p. 179.
2. *Ibid.*, p. 255.
3. Claus Westermann, *Creation* (Philadelphia: Fortress, 1971), p. 109.
4. This position disagrees with the Roman Catholic doctrine, official since 1954, that the Virgin Mary shares this unique quality.

CHAPTER 6. THE MEANS OF JUSTIFICATION

1. George W. Forell, *The Augsburg Confession: A Contemporary Commentary* (Minneapolis: Augsburg, 1968), p. 29.
2. See the Ninety-Five Theses, No. 56-66, esp. 62. In *Luther's Works,* American Edition. Vol. 31, pp. 30-31.
3. Some Lutherans have felt it necessary "to extol the ministry," to speak of some change in nature affected by ordination, and/or to consider ordination a sacrament. See Apol., p. 212. This has never been accepted by the majority of Lutherans, who hold to a functional view of ministry and to the existence of only two sacraments.
4. See my *Reformation Then and Now,* pp. 30-34.
5. *Luther's Works.* American Edition. Vol. 54, p. 92.
6. See their earlier attacks on the opponents for their errors in this connection, p. 46; see also S.A. II, p. 303; L.C., p. 366.
7. Schlink, p. 110.
8. *Luther's Works.* American Edition. Vol. 31, p. 350.

CHAPTER 7. THE RESULTS OF JUSTIFICATION

1. Forell, pp. 32-33.
2. *Luther's Works,* American Edition. Vol. 51, p. 71.
3. *Ibid.,* p. 95.
4. *Ibid.,* Vol. 31, p. 367.
5. *Ibid.,* p. 371.
6. *Ibid.,* p. 368.

For Further Reading

Allbeck, William. *Studies in The Lutheran Confessions.* Rev. ed. Philadelphia: Fortress, 1968.

A revision of a work that appeared in 1952, this study is meant to be a companion piece to the Book of Concord. It treats the materials in the order they appear in the Book of Concord and is helpful in setting the documents in historical context.

Anderson, Charles S. *The Reformation Then and Now.* Minneapolis: Augsburg, 1966.

Helpful in providing brief historical accounts and theological summaries of the major Reformation figures and movements.

Cochran, Arthur, ed. *Reformed Confessions of the Sixteenth Century.* Philadelphia: Westminster, 1966.

Another helpful contextual study. The Lutheran position can only be understood when compared to other statements of the time.

Elert, Werner. *The Structure of Lutheranism.* St. Louis: Concordia, 1962.

An excellent work, helpful for anyone who wishes to understand both the message and form of the Lutheran heritage. The confessions are interpreted historically, and the data of history are interpreted confessionally.

Fagerberg, Holsten. *A New Look at the Lutheran Confessions, 1529-1537*. St. Louis: Concordia, 1972.

This work by a noted Swedish theologian concentrates on the writings of Luther and Melanchthon which have assumed confessional status. The entirety of the Book of Concord is not addressed. Particular care is taken to compare the Confessors' positions with their Roman Catholic and Reformed contemporaries. The close connection between the Confessions and the Scriptures is also underscored.

Forde, Gerhard. *Where God Meets Man*. Minneapolis: Augsburg, 1972.

The most helpful brief summary of Luther's theology of which I am aware.

Forell, George W. *The Augsburg Confession: A Contemporary Commentary*. Minneapolis: Augsburg, 1968.

The author, with characteristic verve, stresses the relevance of the Augsburg Confession for our day.

Kelly, J. N. D. *Early Christian Creeds*. London: Longmans, Green and Co., 1952.

This detailed and scholarly work is of great value in studying the early creeds which became a part of our confessions. It is the best of its type.

Nestingen, James and Forde, Gerhard. *Free to Be—A Handbook to Luther's Small Catechism*. Minneapolis: Augsburg, 1975.

Designed and written as a part of the curriculum of the American Lutheran Church, this study, which has both students' and teachers' texts, fills a need. It moves the catechism into the mainstream of modern life and allows it to speak to our day.

Neve, J. L. *Introduction to the Symbolical Books of the Lutheran Church*. Columbus: Wartburg Press, 1926.

Many church and pastoral libraries will have this text. While out of date, it is helpful and can be used with profit. Other, more recent, titles should also be read.

Schaff, Philip. *Creeds of Christendom*. 3 vols. New York: Harper Press, 1877. Reprint Grand Rapids: Baker Books, n.d.

The most complete presentation of both contents and contexts of the confessions of the Christian community.

Schlink, Edmund. *Theology of the Lutheran Confessions*. Philadelphia: Muhlenberg Press, 1961.

The single most helpful companion volume to a study of the Book of Concord. The current value of the Confessions as witness to the historic Christian faith is continually stressed.

Tappert, Theodore et. al., ed. and trans. *The Book of Concord —The Confessions of the Evangelical Lutheran Church*. Philadelphia: Fortress Press, 1959.

Dr. Tappert and his colleagues, J. Pelikan, R. H. Fischer, and A. C. Piepkorn, have provided an indispensible tool for study of the Lutheran confessional heritage. This is the best English edition of the documents.